MW00463033

Drowning for Jesus

Drowning for Jesus

Compassion Fatigue in Ministry

Jeff and Kathy Hoppe

Foreword by Bill Buker

RESOURCE *Publications* · Eugene, Oregon

DROWNING FOR JESUS
Compassion Fatigue in Ministry

Copyright © 2020 Jeff and Kathy Hoppe. All rights reserved. Except for brief quotations in critical publications or reviews, no part of this book may be reproduced in any manner without prior written permission from the publisher. Write: Permissions, Wipf and Stock Publishers, 199 W. 8th Ave., Suite 3, Eugene, OR 97401.

Resource Publications
An Imprint of Wipf and Stock Publishers
199 W. 8th Ave., Suite 3
Eugene, OR 97401

www.wipfandstock.com

PAPERBACK ISBN: 978-1-7252-8163-9
HARDCOVER ISBN: 978-1-7252-8162-2
EBOOK ISBN: 978-1-7252-8164-6

Manufactured in the U.S.A.   09/17/20

All Scripture quotations, unless otherwise indicated, are taken from the Holy Bible, New International Version®, NIV®. Copyright ©1973, 1978, 1984, 2011 by Biblica, Inc.™ Used by permission of Zondervan. All rights reserved worldwide. www.zondervan.com The "NIV" and "New International Version" are trademarks registered in the United States Patent and Trademark Office by Biblica, Inc.™

The names and case histories of people in this book have been altered to protect the people who shared and to provide anonymity.

We are truly grateful for those who shared their stories as we walked alongside them. We dedicate this to all ministry leaders, pastors, church staff, pastoral caregivers, and ministry spouses who commit themselves to providing care for all God's people. You willingly give your life for the sacrifice of the kingdom. It does not go unnoticed and your reward is waiting for you.

Contents

Foreword

ONE WAY TO DISTINGUISH various types of ministers and ministries is by assessing the distance between them and those to whom they are ministering. Some approaches to helping, such as those primarily using the modalities of television and social media, may have little if any direct contact with the recipients of their ministry whereas others, such as those offering pastoral care and counseling services, have to develop close and in many cases, prolonged contact with those seeking their assistance. While all types of ministry have value, not all exert the same emotional, spiritual, and even physical toll. This difference is especially relevant for those whose services require developing close pastoral/clinical relationships.

Walking compassionately with others through the deepest, darkest, and most disorienting phases of their journey necessitates courage, as well as the capacity to tolerate ambiguity and complexity. Those brave enough to embark on this path of ministry ultimately discover that the process of redemption, though fulfilling at times, is messy and can be draining to the point of depletion and burnout. Learning to practice adequate self-care is critical to maintaining compassion, competence, and longevity in ministry.

Every gift has its shadow side. Although there is little that can compare with the thrill of exercising our gifts to benefit others, there are also many pitfalls to which even seasoned ministers can fall prey if not remaining alert and careful. For instance, every time a caregiver listens deeply to another's story, attempting to understand and empathize with that person's experience, they actually create similar experiences for themselves. In so doing, some of the intensity of the other person's emotions are absorbed, which over time and across situations can have a depleting effect.

This process of empathic connection has been creatively illustrated through use of fMRI images where the brain activity of both the caregiver and care receiver is monitored during their conversations. As caregivers sought to understand the experience of care receivers, who were generally in emotionally distressed states, the caregivers' brains would eventually begin showing activity in the same areas as those of the care receivers, thus indicating that the caregiver was not only understanding the content of the care receiver's message but also having a similar experience. In other words, they were actually feeling, at least to some extent, what the care receiver was feeling.

While this process of hearing and empathizing with the experiences of others is a powerful component of effective caregiving, it exerts its toll. Unless caregivers exercise meaningful self-care, they will be prone to suffering compassion fatigue and, thus, discover it difficult to continue providing the quality of ministry that those who seek their help are craving to find. This is where Jeff and Kathy Hoppe's book becomes a vital resource, especially for those ministers/clinicians who desire to finish strong, rather than just make an impressive start.

Based on expertise gleaned from their extensive experience as caregivers in both pastoral and clinical settings, Jeff and Kathy offer practical wisdom that will benefit both the beginning student and the seasoned professional. They provide a healthy corrective to the seemingly pervasive performance-oriented Christian culture, which often gives the impression that the goal of ministry is to burn out for Jesus, and those who do so the quickest or most dramatically win. As you read their work, I believe you will discover that they not only understand the demands and traps of ministry but also the opportunities and potential. I encourage you to pay close attention to their insights so that you can finish your course with honor and ultimately hear God's validation, "Well done, good and faithful servant."

Bill Buker, DMin, PhD, LPC
Associate Dean, College of Theology and Ministry
Oral Roberts University
June 25, 2020

Preface

WE ARE COMPLETING THIS book on our thirty-ninth anniversary. What a wonderful celebration of life. We met shortly after college and served in student ministry on campuses two hours apart. This afforded us many opportunities for collaboration while driving to meetings together. We had no idea the journey would lead us forty years later to this moment in time when we would share our joys, and yet our struggles along the way. We were young, idealistic, and sure we would change the world. And we did, but not in the way we envisioned. Where we are today is not where we planned. Instead, God's idea was different.

We completed our graduate degrees at the same seminary, and joining our lives in marriage, began seeking ways to serve God. While at seminary, we both volunteered every Friday evening at Marin Suicide Prevention Hotline. The training and service prepared us for ministry in practical ways that theological studies could not. We served as members of First Baptist Church in Sonoma, California, and received unending support for our vocational calling. We have remained in contact with some of those people throughout the years. Kathy completed her first unit of clinical pastoral education at Western State Hospital in Steilacoom, Washington, while at seminary. As she lived on campus with one thousand patients, and worked with mentally ill offenders, it gave her an introduction to working with people who struggle with depression, bipolar disorder, schizophrenia, and other mental illnesses. In the meantime, Jeff volunteered as a chaplain at San Quentin, exposing him to the suffering of those imprisoned.

Upon graduation, we moved to North Dakota as church planters. We started a church, Riverwood Baptist Church, which remains vibrant today. During that time, Kathy completed a second unit of clinical pastoral education at a local hospital and encouraged Jeff to do the same. We were both burning out at the time with the hard work of church planting, and Jeff completed his first unit of clinical pastoral education at a hospital with John Valentino, clinical pastoral educator. It was timely and gave Jeff a fresh view of ministry. In our hospital work, we provided pastoral care to all who entered, those who were hopeful about new births, and new opportunities for life, and those who were grieving. We even learned how deeply grief goes when we lost our second son during that time, but it also gave us a new vision for the future—helping those who are hurting.

We moved to Texas for Jeff to complete a residency program in clinical pastoral education, and when that was done, moved to Tulsa, Oklahoma, where Eleanor Mullins, who was then volunteer manager for a local hospital, saw in Jeff the type of chaplain who could provide services to patients. He was the first full-time chaplain to serve at Tulsa Regional Medical Center. He was the only chaplain working there and on-call twenty-four hours a day. Kathy began her work as a family therapist during this time. She completed a postgraduate program in marriage and family therapy and soon word of her excellent therapy skills led to teaching part-time in the graduate counseling and theology program at Oral Roberts University. Jeff was also gaining attention as he mentored young ministers from the local seminaries as they completed practicums and internships with him. Both of us have watched as our students grew and became even more successful than we could ever achieve.

However, our work was not done. Kathy began experiencing burnout as a mental health professional at about the same time that Jeff was a first responder to the Oklahoma City bombing. Shortly thereafter, Jeff and Kathy attended a weekend workshop on compassion fatigue with Eric Gentry, who had designed an accelerated program of recovery for compassion fatigue in collaboration with Anna Baranowsky and Charles Figley at the Traumatology

Institute in Florida. This was another turning point and led Kathy to complete a doctor of ministry degree with a project on burnout and compassion fatigue in ministry while serving as a hospice chaplain. She continued her education by becoming a certified compassion fatigue professional and educator, and a certified clinical trauma professional. Jeff began his training as a clinical pastoral educator and upon completion, was offered a position as senior director of pastoral care at a Pennsylvania hospital, where he remained for several years. We then moved to New Mexico for five years, serving at hospitals and colleges and hospices. Finally, we returned to our home in Tulsa, where Jeff began working with veterans and continued his work with clinical pastoral education students. During these years, we had many opportunities to serve as interim pastors for small churches.

Throughout the journey, we were privileged to meet and counsel many men and women who served in ministry as pastors, church staff, chaplains, and counselors, all of whom had stories to share of their pain and survival in ministry. We believe we had a part in saving some lives, restoring some careers, and in bringing hope to those pastoral leaders so that they could continue in their vocation. Some have remained in contact with us, many we have lost touch with, but in all we have faith they are finding their way.

In reading the final draft aloud, we could read no further than the introduction to find our emotions rising. We wondered why that stirred us so, and then realized that, in many ways, this manuscript serves as our autobiography. We have touched and have been touched by so many people. We wanted to share the lessons we've learned with you and hope that it provides you with courage and strength. We chose to use the singular voice in our writing to prevent confusion. While the names of the characters and their situations are altered to protect them, the stories are real.

Jonah seems an unlikely biblical character to use for a book on burnout and compassion fatigue. There are others in Scripture who probably fit better. Yet, the inspiration to use Jonah came from Jeff's love of swimming and the ocean. In our reading and studying of Jonah's life, we realized there were many lessons for ministerial leaders in this small book about one part of Jonah's life. We don't know the end of the story, just as we will not know the end of your story. But we trust that you will find solace, and God's quiet whisper to continue in what God is calling you to do.

Blessings, Jeff & Kathy Hoppe

Acknowledgments

WRITING BOOKS IS DONE only with the help of many people. There is never an individual author, but rather many who contribute. We are grateful for all who encouraged and supported us along the way, including those who listened to us talk unendingly about our ideas and those who read chapters and offered feedback.

We are ever so grateful for our experiences in clinical pastoral education (CPE) and how that offered reflection and support when we most needed it. We were not surprised to learn that completing CPE is a protective factor for those in ministry. While CPE is challenging, and at times feels threatening to one's faith and self-construct, we encourage all ministers to complete some time in CPE. To those who shared their stories, thank you for trusting us. We have altered your names and situations to protect you but your narrative rings clear with us. We are thankful to J. Eric Gentry and his work in the field of traumatology. His workshops on compassion fatigue provided us with the launching point in healing our own burnout and compassion fatigue. To our confidants and counselors along the way, we are grateful.

We would like to thank those who work to provide care and counseling to ministry leaders. Tim Reside, CEO of Bright Tomorrows, who has walked this path and whose father walked the path of ministry, and his wife, Nancy, offer such vital support to those who are in the field of ministry. We're also grateful to our dear friend, Jeremy Skaggs, senior pastor of The Welcome Table Christian Church in Arlington, Texas. Jeremy started as a student,

Acknowledgments

then coworker, and now trusted companion in this journey. His encouragement of our ministry is so helpful. We are also thankful to our colleagues at work who are patient with us as we work on these writing projects. To our friend Tom Mathew, a fellow pastoral caregiver and former dean of graduate theology at Oral Roberts University. He trusted us to mentor young people in pastoral care and counseling. We're also thankful for Bill Buker, who has also welcomed us and listened deeply to our stories.

Sometimes there are people who come into your life and you have no idea how deep the friendship will go. Then you find yourself looking back to see they were there with you the entire way. We are broken and wounded people, and it would be logical to leave us to live out that frailty, along with our many mistakes. But these trusted people have never left us no matter what happened. They maintained connection, prayer, and offered good meals with lots of laughter along the way. Thank you to our dear friends Tim and Diane Peterson, Dave and Gwen Fleske, John and Joy Valentino, and Teri Burnett for always staying present for us.

Last, but never, ever least, are our children. Our sons grew up in the world of ministry, knowing what ministry children experience, and sometimes being privy to information that was a burden to bear. We love you and are so proud of the men you have become. We pray that you will continue to hear God's call to you in your chosen vocations.

Introduction

Swim at Your Own Risk

They will stretch out their hands in it,
as swimmers stretch their hands to swim.

—ISAIAH 25:11

SWIMMING IS AS NATURAL as breathing to me. I played in the sea during childhood and adolescence. Life in Freeport, Grand Bahama, gave me an opportunity to explore the expansive ocean. Attending school in a uniform was restrictive, so when the bell rang, I ran home fast to slip into my favorite swim trunks and plunge into the nearest tide. Floating on my back, I noticed the sounds disappeared. I would dive deeper and search the coral reef looking for treasures. Marine life was captivating. I saw surgeon-fish with their sharp blades, tough damselfish, parrotfish, slow-moving pufferfish that suck in and swell up like comical balloons, angelfish, seahorses, stingrays, and turtles. I swam over urchins, sponges, and hermit crabs. My mother and I collected seashells. Mom kept one large conch shell into my adulthood, and I could hold it to my ear and still hear the waves.

Moving to Florida as a teen, I joined the high school aquatic team. In competition, I learned to use the pool's edges to my advantage for a quick send-off and return. But the lure of the ocean was always in my head. The sea was near where I encountered the slow-moving manatee, playful dolphins, and egrets, terns, herons, and pelicans. My love of water remains with me to this day.

Ocean swimming differs from pools. They are distinct places. The pool has sides, no waves unless someone jumps in, and no creatures to avoid or observe, whereas the ocean gives me little control. Sea creatures drift into my path, some who are friendly while others are not so pleasant. The currents change with little warning. A pool has edges for safety; the ocean's safest place is the beach. I always keep land in sight. While a swimming pool can be dangerous, it does not compare to the safety issues that one confronts in an open sea.

In open waters, there are times when fear grips me. A wave rises high, an undercurrent pulls me downward, or a storm brews, bringing high winds. In a few minutes, the entire ocean changes from a friendly and relaxing place to a violent and frightful one. I am a solid swimmer, able to perform a variety of strokes, but there are situations that challenge my skills. I've learned to listen to the ocean and adjust my body, mind, and choices based upon her fluctuations.

Through the years, I continue to find places to swim in lakes, seas, or natural bodies of water. Enormous signs loom at some entrances: *Swim at Your Own Risk.* I understand what that means. The warning reminds everyone the swimming hole could be unsafe. I consider these alerts, knowing someone more familiar with this spot knows of the potential perils. While I love the water, I understand the respect it demands. A person can get in trouble in an ocean.

Ministry is much the same. In our roles as educators, ministers, and counselors, we offer a lifeline to those people who are drowning in the demands of religious careers. Similar to pristine waters, the allure of spiritual leadership teases one into service. As the tide changes, the winds of demands and expectations swell high, ready to crash upon ministers trying to keep afloat. Just like the ocean, one can expect turbulence. But leaders may not notice the subtle change in currents that will pull them to depths that place them at risk.

Years spent in education prepare the ministry leader with biblical knowledge and a solid theological foundation. While a few courses teach pastoral care and church administration, little emphasis is on the practical knowledge needed to thrive in religious settings. Upon graduation, many pastoral leaders move to church settings. Few will start as senior pastors of large congregations. Most will arrive at small parishes that understand better how to survive time compared to the idealist who comes to change the world. It's a training ground for the new pastor, and churches are aware of this.

We work with ministry staff and their spouses to regain equilibrium and revitalize their careers and families. This book describes our experiences, training, and research. We also include brief stories from those whom we helped. We want to protect these people, so the names, dates, and situations have been altered to provide them anonymity while letting their voices speak. There are three primary segments in this book. The titles of the sections support the allegory of swimming or sea life, based on Jonah's struggle in his spiritual calling. The first section, "The Beckoning Sea," discusses the calling to ministry and the inherent perils. Part 2, "Finding Your Stroke," explores the personal characteristics that place leaders at risk and discusses ways to prevent burnout and compassion fatigue. In part 3, "The Rescue," we explain the path to recovery and continuing ministry development. After each chapter, we offer reflective questions. We urge you to take a moment to read those and examine your place in ministry. If you read this material without practicing or using the tools, you may remain at risk. Using good information, forming fresh ways of thinking, and developing solid skills will keep you from drowning. Better yet, you may learn to love swimming!

Part I

The Beckoning Sea

The word of the Lord came to Jonah son of Amittai:
"Go to the great city of Nineveh and preach against it,
because its wickedness has come up before me."

—JONAH 1:1-2

THE OCEAN IS ENTICING. I remember my first trip to Hawaii. I couldn't wait to get in the water. I just wanted to touch and taste it and feel it envelop me. Water is a mystery that I can experience. I don't understand it, but I'm drawn to it. Whether an ocean, a lake, a stream, or a waterfall, I cannot pass it without putting my hand or foot in it. Yet that's not enough, I want to go deep into it until I am surrounded by the quiet. Water is hypnotizing; it draws me near. Imagine the thrill I felt on Hawaii's north shore as the waves crashed against my body. The smells, the sounds, and the feel of the spray are as real to me now as they were at the time of my visit. Whenever I am stressed, I close my eyes and revisit the ocean to gain a sense of steadiness and calm. The water's beckoning is inescapable for me.

Just like the thrill of ocean swimming, such is God's calling on your life. Few other professions have that grip on an individual. A person typically opts for a career that fits his or her aptitude or interests. If a person is good at math throughout school, then likely he or she will pursue a career that uses those skills. For the person interested in humanities, a probable career choice might be in social services, teaching, or even the law. The person who loves science will enter the sciences, engineering, or medical field. Rarely do I hear people in other careers use the sense of mission as a minister uses it. At one point, someone asked me, "Why do you want to be a minister?" I hesitated and then replied, "Oh, I don't *want* to be a minister. God called me. How can I choose otherwise?" No other career incorporates one's entire soul such as ministry.

The call of God is powerful. It harbors both the possibility of great joy in serving God and the church, and yet ramifications, should you resist the invitation. The story of Jonah shows what happens when one disobeys God's command to serve. When God decides to choose a person for ministry, the invitation is appealing. In his book *Testing and Reclaiming Your Call*, Robert Schnase writes, "The mystery we wrestle with is that God wishes to use any of us at all. Of all the strange ways for God to reveal unlimited love, God uses limited lives."[1] It seems odd that such an auspicious task is given to you, an ordinary being who is limited in knowledge and vulnerable to pride, discouragement, disillusionment, and exhaustion. At the same time, it's appealing to consider that you are deemed worthy to serve the Almighty.

God demonstrates grace toward humanity by entrusting the gospel message to you. Your response to this call is unpredictable. How you react involves the tension between autonomy and surrender. If you rely on your own strength and desires, the path becomes draining, and eventually may lead to burnout or compassion fatigue. It is a career that requires a dependency upon God and a continual reevaluation of your theological belief system. The calling to ministry awakens, motivates, encourages, and strengthens you. It is this vocation that sustains you through difficult times. Eugene Peterson describes this assurance, "It suddenly struck me

1. Schnase, *Testing*, 42.

that my ordination vows had functioned for the past forty years as pitons, pegs driven firmly into the vertical rock face upon which Christian ministry is played out."[2]

Yet God gives you freedom to respond. The personal responsibility that comes with the vow will remain with you and the commitment of that initiative becomes apparent amid trouble.[3] Spiritual vocation demands a pledge that you may not always be ready to make. Consider the resistance of the biblical characters. In Exodus 3, God speaks to Moses. "I am sending you to Pharaoh to bring my people the Israelites out of Egypt." What is Moses's response? "Who am I that I should go to Pharaoh and bring the Israelites out of Egypt?"[4] Moses argues with God and raises five objections to God's request: I'm not a good enough, I don't have the answers, the people won't believe me, I'm not a good speaker, and I'm not a leader.[5] Jeremiah's story is similar. "The word of the Lord came to me, saying, 'Before I formed you in the womb I knew you, before you were born I set you apart; I appointed you as a prophet to the nations.' 'Alas, Sovereign Lord,' I said, 'I do not know how to speak; I am too young.'"[6]

The response to God's bid is one of awe and bewilderment that soon turns to excitement and wonder. Many enter the pastoral field with high hopes and large expectations of themselves. The clergy life holds both possibilities and challenges, opportunities for growth and moments of doubt, and intense satisfaction and great disappointment. Church leaders throughout history comment on the hard work of ministry. Gregory of Nazianzus left the profession because shepherding people was harder than guiding a flock of sheep.[7] Chrysostom stated the task of ministry was

---

2. Dawn and Peterson, *Unnecessary Pastor*, 13.

3. Childs, *Book of Exodus*, 73.

4. Exod 3:10–11.

5. Exod 3:11–15.

6. Jer 1:4–6.

7. Tidball, *Skillful Shepherds*, 155.

overwhelming.[8] Spurgeon remarked that pastoral caregiving was a great burden to bear.[9]

Ministry can be difficult, and the affirmation of a calling is imperative. In his book *The Preacher, His Life and Work*, John Jowett makes this clear:

> I hold a profound conviction that before a man selects the Christian ministry as his vocation he must have the assurance that the selection has been imperatively constrained by the eternal God. The call of the Eternal must ring through the rooms of his soul as clearly as the sound of the morning bell rings through the valleys of Switzerland, calling the peasants to early prayer and praise.[10]

Spurgeon warned those who were uncertain of their calling to wait until certainty arrived.[11] The appeal must be carefully considered. There is a cost to hearing God's voice. Once called, your life is never the same. It requires relinquishment of what you desire in responding to the Holy One. You will be tested and must have an ongoing sense of your spiritual vocation to avoid losing heart.

Perhaps Jonah understands the potential pitfalls. From the beginning, Jonah understands what this mission entails, and that's why he refuses. There are some pastors who do not understand what they're getting into when they accept a call to a particular church. It doesn't matter how many theology classes one takes, or how much knowledge of Greek or Hebrew one possesses, or even one's biblical expertise. The clergy accepting a church bid have no foresight of the problems they will face. Even when informed, their idealism prevents them from seeing the potential dilemmas ahead. The seminary sends the graduates out in a dinghy on a calm sea. The new ministers have no idea what's about to swallow them.

---

8. Tidball, *Skillful Shepherds*, 155.

9. Spurgeon, *All Round Ministry*, 214.

10. Jowett, *Preacher*, 12.

11. Spurgeon, *All Round Ministry*, 13.

Chapter 1

Diving without Looking

But Jonah ran away from the Lord and headed for Tarshish.
He went down to Joppa, where he found a ship bound for that port.
After paying the fare, he went aboard and sailed
for Tarshish to flee from the Lord.

—JONAH 1:3

FEW CHARACTERS ARE AS fascinating as Jonah. The reluctant prophet tries to escape God's calling. He buys a boat ticket in his effort to run away. Hiding in his room below deck while the sea rages, the sailors find him and drag him to the upper deck. Accusing Jonah of creating the storm, they ask for an explanation. Seeking to undo the dilemma, and further escape God's bidding, Jonah has the sailors throw him overboard. One might think Jonah is altruistic in his effort to save the crew and passengers from the sea gales, but let's be honest. He's running from God. His evasion doesn't stop there; we see his resistance throughout the story. Once he's in the belly of an enormous fish, and he's still alive, he pleads for rescue. Who wouldn't? His bargaining with the Almighty One sends him straight to Nineveh, a city full of sinners, just where God told him to go. This is a lesson for those trying to circumvent their calling. But I'm getting ahead of myself. The point I want you to see is not Jonah's anger or foolish decisions. I think Jonah has an awareness that I wish all ministers might have.

Religious service comes with unique problems that few other career paths meet. These include expansive roles, high expectations, diffuse boundaries, and power dynamics. The minister may have a vague awareness of these demands. But how this plays out in church systems is obscure until the leader moves into the office, enjoys the welcome potluck, and preaches the first sermon. The waters are calm, and swimming is smooth. Still, the winds and tides will turn, and even the most experienced ministry leader will struggle with the ensuing squall.

The Perils of Ministry

The first five years of religious service determine whether clergy stay in the ministry. In a study of five thousand clergy, 75 percent of the ministers say they are struggling with the tasks, and 50 percent think of leaving the field.[1] Other ministers speak of exhaustion. Some define their depleted experience as compassion fatigue. This stress syndrome occurs because of both systemic and personal factors. In addition, pastors are called to perform counseling services. According to Weaver and colleagues, clergy report spending 15 percent of their work time providing pastoral counseling[2] without the formal training that mental health professionals receive. Commonly, clergy are the first line of defense when parishioners experience trauma, placing the minister at risk for vicarious traumatization.[3] While pastors report feeling competent regarding issues of grief, anxiety, and marriage problems, they report feeling less able to provide effective services to those congregants with severe mental illness, depression, substance abuse,

1. Abernethy et al., "Pastors Empowerment Program," 177.
2. Weaver et al., "Collaboration," 163.
3. Noullet et al., "Effect of Pastoral Crisis," 1.

or who are suicidal.[4] Yet churches expect leaders to provide such pastoral care. Among the ministers with whom I work, the sense of drowning is common, yet it's unnecessary.

Stephen and his wife, Denise, moved into the area, full of hope and expectation. Excited about his first church, Stephen had many ideas of how to enhance church growth. Since we were colleagues, we talked frequently. After six months, Stephen came to talk about managing the church politics. This was something he hadn't expected. His honeymoon was ending despite his best efforts in leading the congregation. He was energetic, outgoing, and a good orator. Susan was friendly but hesitant to dive deeply into church life. She wanted to set boundaries, especially since they lived next door to the church. While thankful for the enormous parsonage, she and Stephen were uncomfortable with how freely members stopped by and expected a hospitable welcome. Stephen and Susan stayed at the church for two years. That was enough for both. Stephen changed careers and became an insurance agent. Disappointed with the experience, their involvement with church was never the same again. A few years later, I sadly learned of their impending divorce, of which both attributed to the rocky start at church ministry and the ensuing demands. They were a bright couple who had a lot to offer to the church but were unable to manage the beginning travails of ministry.

The Role of Clergy

Your role as a pastor or leader is complex. While other jobs have clear descriptions with assigned requisites, specified hours for working, and separation of personal life from work life, the ministry does not. You serve in many ways, including preaching, teaching, administration, counseling, and pastoral care. You may also act as volunteer coordinator, fundraiser, marketer, evangelist, and supervisor. In some situations, you may be the janitor, landscaper, crisis counselor, and even miracle worker or any other tasks

4. Jacobson et al., "Risk for Burnout," 456.

the church deems necessary. The role of risk assessment or case manager increases your risk for compassion fatigue.[5] Before one duty is complete, another will demand attention, an emergency will arise, and a former issue will resurface. You keep a job list, complete one chore, and add three more. The work is draining and places you at risk for burnout.

While working with leaders of one church, I realized they might have difficulty finding a pastor to fit their ministry vision. The church loved their former minister, Paul, because of his eloquence and acts of service to the people. He was single, well-educated, charismatic, and grew up in the church. Paul's parents also attended the church and taught him well how to care for others. He visited people in trouble in the middle of the night, bringing milk, toiletries, or any other items requested. He spent time with high school students, often tutoring them and aiding them with homework. Paul's resignation came with tears but promises that he was always welcome to return. When a new pastor, Bill, arrived, he couldn't keep pace with the expectations. He was married, middle-aged, and tried to set boundaries around his personal and home life. Bill wasn't free at two in the morning to buy someone a candy bar. The church could not adjust to Bill and his family, so the congregation voted Bill out the following year with an inadequate amount of time to show his ministry talents.

The Expectations

Along with many chores, you operate amid high expectations. Dane Aaker says, "As a pastor you are bombarded with demoralizing criticism and intoxicating praise."[6] There are values placed upon production, including baptisms, membership, financial solvency, and visitation. The church ties the results to your performance, which influences your longevity. While tenure is

---

5. Abernethy et al., "Pastors Empowerment Program," 177.

6. Aaker, "Church Bizarre," 1.

increasing, it remains about four to six years for most pastors.[7] The third year is critical because that's when most pastors leave the church.[8] It's as if you are working on commission and must become the premier salesperson, except without the reciprocal compensation and benefits.

Marian serves as a pastor of a church with fewer than a hundred people. She came to the church five years ago. Her salary has not increased, and she pays for her own insurance. Marian's church is about seventy-five years old, and its attendance has declined through the years. She says, "I've tried everything. I visit people, take part in community events, and volunteer at every opportunity. But no one seems to notice. The town population is decreasing, and that affects our church. How do you grow a church in a town that's dying?" Yet, Marian comes to counseling as required by her denomination for poor performance. It is unlikely the church district will move her to a better functioning congregation, despite her best efforts to succeed in a dismal situation. She will have to grapple with trying to improve or resign from her ministry position.

Pastoring is not an eight-hour job. The person entering ministry must understand the job requires working on weekends, being on call day and night, and frequent interruptions. Most pastors understand the need for accessibility and offer themselves to their congregants. This leads to permeable boundaries wherein church and personal life overlap, and daily intrusions into a pastor's time and family are frequent. This can overwhelm the minister and his or her spouse. Dan, an associate pastor of a medium-sized church, came seeking help. "I'm frustrated with my church. My wife is upset with me. The demands on my time are constant. If I try to take a day off, someone has a crisis, and I get called anyway. I don't know how to handle all of this."

7. Rainer, "Dangerous Third Year," 1.
8. Rainer, "Seven Reasons," 1.

The Dynamics of Organizations

Those who respond to church bids are unaware of the political dynamics present in a church setting. The best advice I received from an experienced pastor was, "When you start at a church, look for the power structure." In some churches, the polity and practice are clear, and the minister knows where the decision-making power lies. But there is a covert system at work that influences this body, and it will affect the pastor. Our friend Eric learned this the hard way. Upon arrival at his new church, a welcoming group brought groceries and greeted Eric, helped his family unpack their belongings, and even took the kids to a playground so Eric and his wife could settle in. These people, a husband and wife, Jim and Sally, along with a deacon, Derek, praised Eric publicly, bragging on his pastoral presence. While not part of the church board, they were active members whom Eric appreciated. He found it easy to confide in Jim and Sally. Eric had little understanding that everything he said was repeated to various board members, and he was being tested on a regular basis. When Eric was called into a monthly meeting to face allegations of insubordination to the church board, he was shocked. While the board supported Eric, he was reprimanded and reminded that he was fortunate to get such a wonderful position in a vibrant congregation. From that point forward, Eric trusted no one. This power dynamic is real. The leader needs the skill to find who influences vital decisions and learn to work within that system.

Too often ministers embark on the ministry career with little understanding of the perils of ministry life, a lack of self-awareness, poor preparation to manage the mental health concerns of the congregants and arrive at the parish with wishful hopes and dreams. Grosch and Olsen say,

> Most clergy began their careers with high ideals, enormous optimism, idealism about their ability to be helpful, and a commitment to help people. They believed that the right combination of quality training, compassion, and commitment would enable them to bring healing to a

wide variety of individuals. They entered the field not to make money, but to help as many individuals as possible.[9]

People responding to the call of God to pastoral ministry soon experience a vision conflict. What they experience in service to the church rarely matches what they anticipated.[10] Soon leaders will face a decreasing sense of satisfaction along with a diminishing loss of meaning and confusion about their calling.[11]

Like our friend Eric, the ministry will place stress upon you through conflict, overload, poor boundaries, and loss of hope for positive change.[12] If Eric can find a way to change his interactions with the church and improve his self-management, and if he can endure for a few more years, he can likely experience increasing satisfaction that will sustain him in ministry. Clergy with more tenure learn the necessary coping skills to adapt to the work and eventually experience less burnout.[13] That's our hope for Eric. I hope this information provides you with alertness, so you will look before diving into ministry or before entering a particular setting. In the following chapters I offer a deeper discussion of systemic factors that influence your ministry, the faulty survival techniques that pull you down, and the symptoms of burnout and compassion fatigue.

Reflection

Take some time to reflect on the following questions:

1. In this chapter I state, "When God decides to choose a person for ministry, the beckoning is ceaseless." In what ways is this statement true for you?

---

9. Grosch and Olsen, "Clergy Burnout," 619.
10. Spencer et al., "Predicting," 92.
11. Spencer et al., "Predicting the Level of Pastors' Risk," 93.
12. Spencer et al., "Predicting the Level of Pastors' Risk," 85.
13. Jacobson et al., "Risk for Burnout," 457.

2. How have you experienced the dynamic of tension between personal autonomy and dependence on the Divine?

3. What has been the most exhausting aspect(s) of your ministry journey?

4. I state, "The role of pastor is complex." In what ways is this true for you?

Imagine viewing your response to God's calling on your life to ministry as a business transaction. Then respond to the following questions:

1. What are some of the explicit/implicit agreements in this covenant?

2. What surprises have you encountered?

"The ministering person is like Sisyphus in Greek mythology, whose fate it was to have to push a great stone up a mountain only to have it roll down again just before reaching the top."[14]

---

14. Sanford, *Ministry Burnout*, 6.

Chapter 2

Barracudas in the Water

Then the sailors said to each other, "Come, let us cast lots
to find out who is responsible for this calamity."
They cast lots and the lot fell on Jonah.

—JONAH 1:7

IF YOU WANT TO view active oceanic life, then snorkeling is an excellent way to do so. Most people play in the water or float on top. Yet it's in diving below the surface that you can observe schools of fish, large sea turtles, and striking plants. It's beautiful to behold and comes with surprises. An example of this is the barracuda. It's a long, tubular fish that's bluish in tint with a pointed snout. It will spring up out of nowhere and open its mouth to reveal two rows of sharp teeth. Getting caught in that jaw would be unpleasant. The barracuda is fast, bursting in speeds up to thirty-five miles per hour with its enormous body sometimes over five feet long and over one hundred pounds. The fish is an ambush hunter, waiting quietly in the water until it sees something interesting, and then attacking at full speed.[1] Listen to Ruth's encounter with a barracuda.

1. Bester, "Sphyraena Barracuda," 1.

> I looked down one time and noticed something get-
> ting bigger, and then something shot past me! I looked
> around feeling disorientated and I came face-to-face
> with this fish. This is a barracuda, as big as I am—and it
> has this unnerving habit of coming right into your face
> and looking at you. I'm looking deep in its gigantic eyes,
> he's looking at me, and of course I'm a bit afraid.[2]

Ruth completes her story by describing her move from fear to awe of the barracuda's beauty. In this transition, she can see the menace as God's creation, and marvels at the privilege of witnessing the fish in action. The barracuda rarely attacks humans. However, shiny objects attract the barracuda; thinking a tasty little fish delight may be attached, it will sneak up and then rapidly grab whatever is attached to the glistening item.[3] That's when you hope that you are not the thing that is sparkling. The barracuda is a possible risk to the diver.

The barracuda scenario represents what you potentially face going into an unfamiliar church setting. There is a life-sustaining environment unknown by you and full of unseen challenges. It's not a danger that threatens your career, but your lack of understanding of the systemic qualities can ambush you. In her work in burnout, Maslach determined that systems are as responsible for burning people out as much as individual characteristics. No matter how much self-care you practice, if you are placed in a structure with certain negative conditions, you will be at risk for burnout or compassion fatigue. "The overall findings from several decades of burnout research have found that situational and environmental factors seem to be as important for understanding burnout as are personal variables."[4]

Such variables include work overload, lack of control over your work, ambiguous roles, insufficient or sporadic rewards, and mismatch of your style, personality, values or beliefs with

---

2. Bancewicz, "In the Eye of the Barracuda," 1.

3. Bester, "Sphyraena Barracuda," 1.

4. Maslach, "Finding Solutions," 145.

the organization.[5] Churches are born and become self-sustaining forces through the use of principles in which all systems thrive. Therapists refer to this as societal emotional process.[6] The church operates as a large family and so family system principles apply. The primary obstacles that you will face lie in homeostasis (how a church maintains balance), triangulation (how the church manages anxiety), family projection and transmission process (how a church family communicates values), and differentiation of self (ability to maintain a sound leadership position within the system).[7] I will break these down and consider how each play a part in ensnaring you.

How Churches Stay in Balance

Every organization, family, or church operates on a feedback loop. Think about your home environment. If you have central heating and air, you're accustomed to setting the thermostat at your preferred temperature and one in which you are most comfortable, or perhaps save money. It's affordable to keep your thermostat at an even level rather than frequently adjusting the temperature, but that requires a feedback system. You set the thermostat, and a sensor inside the thermostat determines if the air temperature is too cool or too warm. If too cool, then the thermostat sends a message to the heating system to turn on until the temperature rises to the preset condition. Once it reaches that level, the thermostat signals the heating system to turn off or decrease its output. It works the same way with the cooling system. There's a continual process of sensing the atmosphere and communicating with the heating and cooling system. It's a feedback loop meant to maintain the temperature you desire. This process is homeostasis.[8]

---

5. Jacobson, "Risk for Burnout," 457.
6. Kerr, *One Family's Story*, loc. 540.
7. Kerr, *One Family's Story*, loc. 58.
8. Kerr, *One Family's Story*, loc. 266.

The same is true in churches. The congregation has a comfortable operating zone of emotional temperature. Too cool, meaning little congregational effort and too much distancing, and the church loses energy, members, and will face closure. Too hot, or rather too many unresolved issues or unbearable conflicts, and the church implodes. Just like the thermostat in a home, the church has a feedback loop, or communication system, that senses when the environment and emotional tone of the church are moving beyond the "preset" or comfortable zone. The feedback loops are the overt methods of church management, i.e., the board, the deacons, etc., and the covert, or unseen efforts such as triangulation or family projection and transmission. The church system attempts to maintain "normal," or homeostasis. That means the church will react to any change introduced, even positive ones, and will strive to return to normal functioning.[9]

Even calling you as a new minister, and the departure of the former pastor, creates an unstable system. Hiring you is the church's effort to reach homeostasis again. That's why the church "settles down" temporarily when you are soundly in place. It's a communal sigh of relief until your interactions with the church increase. The church is working to survive but introducing unfamiliar elements into the system throws the church off balance. And those congregants who are uncomfortable with change, or those who consider themselves defenders of the faith, or gatekeepers for the church, become like barracudas searching for the nurturing food that will rebalance the system. If you attempt church alterations too soon, you become like the shiny object. While the barracudas do not intend to attack you, the result is the sacrifice of your ministry for the sake of homeostasis.

James is a bright seminarian winning many awards for his preaching and so a church choosing him over other candidates is an ego stroke. Confident he can lead this congregation to new growth, he eagerly accepts the call. The parishioners warmly greet James and his wife and introduce him to the community with accolades. He is now a community leader. Things start well. His

---

9. Friedman, *Generation to Generation*, 202–3.

sermons are polished and well-received, creating an increase in church attendance. After a year, James implements some changes in the church that he thinks will contemporize the worship. He introduces a praise team and praise choruses. Such a change does not require a vote of the congregation. James mentions the change in the monthly board meeting and then organizes the transition. Several members are excited, especially those who have visited or moved from churches with contemporary worship. He recruits singers to join the praise team. These new plans require moving items around the front stage of the church. The secretary refashions the church bulletin. James is pleased with the progress.

The transition comes within a few months. The staging is gorgeous as the tech team operates the lighting, sound system, and the slideshow. The praise team leads the congregation in the choruses and the singing is hearty. James swells with pride at this change he successfully implemented. However, he is unaware of the undertone of discomfort and the side conversations among long-term members. "Who does he think he is—changing everything?" "My dad bought that organ to be used every Sunday and now it's just sitting there." "I think Pastor James has a good idea, but he should have asked us first." While the church members enjoy the increase in energy and attendance, this incident sets the stage later for a confrontation when James attempts his next idea.

Every change that comes into church life destabilizes the congregation, even those that affect you personally or your family. Some churches adapt while others become unbalanced. The target naturally becomes you, the leader. And the church system will take significant effort to either shape you to fit the system or expel you as the one who is creating disharmony. It's not personal; it's survival for the system. Many churches persist for twenty, forty, or even more than a hundred years because of the innate ability to either maintain homeostasis or adapt to a new normal. When change is successful, the system will move to protect and maintain the new emotional temperature. One way the system achieves this goal is through triangulation.

Communication Patterns

When Murray Bowen was developing his theory of family systems through his observations of families, he noticed a common occurrence. Whenever conflict between two individuals occurred, such as between husband and wife, the relationship bond experienced increasing anxiety. The couple subconsciously faced a choice, either separating or minimizing the current fear. The natural way to decrease the anxiety was to involve a third person so the anxiety could spread, and each person carry less stress. Bowen and Kerr say, "This involvement of a third person decreases anxiety in the twosome by spreading it through three relationships. . . . This shifting reduces the possibility of any one relationship emotionally 'overheating.' The ability to spread and shift tension, as well as to contain more of it, means that a triangle is more flexible and stable than a two-person system."[10] Think of it like a three-legged stool which can bear more weight than one with two legs. Including a third party displaces the apprehension, up to a point. However, it also means that communication may become indirect and dysfunctional.

In any church, you don't have to look far to find this pattern. When a person is unhappy with you, they inevitably will tell someone else first, rather than having a frank conversation with you. Likewise, you may engage in triangulation when you involve a third person to "gain a better understanding" of a congregant's behavior or words. Peter Steinke explains it, "For any conflict to continue and get out of control, a generator of anxiety and an amplifier are needed. They feed on each other."[11] When two people disagree, or experience anxiety in a relationship, it is common for one to be a generator, the one pulling another party into the situation, and the second person to be an amplifier. "We become amplifiers when we talk about people instead of to people. We take the conflicts other people generate and inadvertently spread them. Sometimes we do this because of our own anticipatory anxiety about the

---

10. Kerr and Bowen, *Family Evaluation*, 135.

11. Steinke, *Congregational Leadership*, 110.

situation. We talk about the generator because we think it might help to protect us if the conflict is amplified."[12]

Sometimes the difficulty does not rest with you but with two congregants or two groups of people within the church. You unwarily step in to mediate or offer peace between the two, only to find this protective act creates an emotional triangle that jeopardizes your leadership.[13] The focus shifts from the two parties onto you. It functions to spread the anxiety among all constituents but leaves the primary issue unresolved. Reeves warns pastors with the following: "Ministers can be hooked into the hero role, which may seem appealing at first. But in the drama of heroes and villains, to remain the hero becomes a high-wire act. Indeed, if you fail at being the hero, your next role: villain."[14]

You may inadvertently step into a triangle, or parishioners may pull you in, either innocently or through manipulation. Triangulation is a common trap for leaders. The Pharisees attempted it with Jesus in Matthew when asking about taxes.

> Then the Pharisees went out and laid plans to trap him in his words. They sent their disciples to him along with the Herodians. "Teacher," they said, "we know that you are a man of integrity and that you teach the way of God in accordance with the truth. You aren't swayed by others, because you pay no attention to who they are. Tell us then, what is your opinion? Is it right to pay the poll-tax to Caesar or not?" But Jesus, knowing their evil intent, said, "You hypocrites, why are you trying to trap me?"[15]

In this passage, the Pharisees intentionally try to discredit Jesus by offering a double bind. Think of Jesus's options. Even in the initial address, the Pharisees disingenuously compliment Jesus. Then they pose a question to triangulate him. Will he oppose the Roman government, committing a rebellious crime, or will he oppose the way of God, proving himself a heretic? However, Jesus

12. Bixby, *Navigating the Nonsense*, 11.

13. Bixby, *Navigating the Nonsense*, 8.

14. Reeves, *Whole Church*, 24.

15. Matt 22:15–18.

is aware of the tactic and de-triangulates himself. If you are oblivious of these interactive patterns, you may unknowingly step on a relationship land mine. It may be sudden or months later before you realize what happened.

It is important to understand that triangulation occurs not only in relationships but with resources. When your wages are tied to baptisms or new members, the triangle shifts. Triangles may comprise you as the minister, the members, and any resource valuable to the church or you, such as financial contribution or pastoral benefits. Let's consider the little community church with wealthy members. Mr. Stoltz and his family formed the congregation over seventy-five years ago. He welcomes the pastor, arrives early with the Sunday donuts, and gives sacrificially until the pastor does something that is disagreeable. Then the funds abruptly stop, the minister's salary is placed on hold, or the contract is not renewed. Ministers serving this small church learn, some too late, that survival means pleasing the power brokers.

Some churches have healthier communication systems while others are more dysfunctional. It's tough to know that ahead of time unless you have a substantial history of the congregation. Part of the information needed includes the church's developmental history including the successes, failures, stresses, and times when wounding occurred. All of this informs you about the family projection and transmission process that sustain the church system.

Family Process

No matter what church you enter, there is a rich history of how the congregation evolved with stories of success and failure. When you look around the building, you will see symbols of that narrative. In the sanctuary the instruments, the décor, and the arrangement represent the collective bargaining of the members. The choice of hymnals, stained glass windows, and additions to the space call forth memories of negotiation. It's easy to surmise that those decisions were logical and governed by church polity. But making that determination is a failure to recognize the deeper processes

of church life. Churches arise from relationship
tainability. The astute clergy person recognizes
structures in the church: those present with eac
families, and within the minister's family. It's a c
interlocking relationships.[16] Armour and Brown

> Once you see the church as an intricate intera
> trapersonal and interpersonal systems, you will avoid the
> mistake of explaining congregational tension in simple
> cause-and-effect terms. Instead, you will see the church
> as an extensive array of highly dynamic, interlocking
> processes. You will know how to delve into those pro-
> cesses and probe beneath the surface, where unspoken
> and unrecognized agendas are often at work.[17]

Churches develop patterns of emotional functioning that influence how members relate to one another, to you as the pastor,
and to stress or anxiety. Much like a family business, churches develop interactions in their efforts to grow and remain functional.
It's a process of negotiation as founders determine what the important tenets and polity will be that require implicit obligation.[18]
The system is built to provide safety for those who are allegiant to
the foundational beliefs and hopes. It must overcome any present
or future barriers or threats to ensure the system's survival. David
Odom reminds us, "Nearly all congregations have informal processes that have developed over years and are rarely explained to
outsiders. It is not surprising that pastors would have trouble dis-
cerning how to make a difference in this complex social system."[19]

While some expectations for how churches operate are explained in the rules or orders, the manner in which it all occurs
remains hidden. Instead, that information is relayed through a pro-
jective transmission process. Those who are elected leaders, those
who have political influence upon leaders, those who have influence
but from a distance, for example, the former deacon who moved

16. Friedman, *Generation to Generation*, 1.

17. Armour and Browning, *Systems-Sensitive Leadership*, 9.

18. Reeves, *Whole Church*, 28.

19. Odom, "Dave Odom," 1.

ay but remains in contact, or a former pastor who continues to advise lay leaders on church matters, and the deceased members who formed and protected the church and whose legacy is defended by current members, determine the direction of the congregation.[20] If you implement change before joining the system, you will experience turbulence. Stevens and Collins say, "The Christian leader can never assume she is an integral part of the group (system) until she has passed through several stages of negotiating acceptance by the congregation."[21] You cannot force your way into the system. It occurs over time as you become entrusted into the congregation. That happens gradually as you support the organization's effort in maintaining and enhancing the church identity. When you do not understand the projection and transmission process, you will find yourself on the outside, with little to shelter you from the natural self-protective tendencies of the congregation. Then you become an unacceptable object that threatens the life of the church. Like the proverbial frog in a pot of water, you may have little awareness that the fire burning beneath will soon erupt around you. Your salvation lies in your level of differentiation.

Leadership Patterns

Pastors are often shocked at how harmful parishioners can be. Unfair criticism, verbal attacks, and reputation assaults are more common than one might imagine. "I know pastors who have experienced their greatest supporters becoming their harshest critics."[22] While leaders can expect that they will have solid supporters, they must anticipate those who will betray them, even in small ways. Jesus's life provides the examples of this abandonment in Judas, Peter, and the other disciples. Even if the betrayal is temporary, it is deeply wounding. The pastor who recognizes these attacks as symptoms of fear and remains a non-anxious presence will fare better.

20. Nessan, "Surviving Congregational Leadership," 391.

21. Stevens and Collins, *Equipping Pastor*, 10.

22. Bishop, "I Was Betrayed," 1.

However, many people new to ministry life desire to please their church and will do whatever is necessary to accomplish that. Little do they realize this mistake will prove costly. Typically, leaders will attempt this through a charismatic personality, their personal magnetism, or through consensus. While attractive and well-spoken leaders can bring dramatic change, they also have a tendency to polarize people, drawing like-minded followers while repelling those who are not like them. They tend to over-function by bearing the anxiety of the system in their efforts to maintain that charisma. This leadership works well in helpless systems that need constant encouragement from a strong leader.[23] The minister who focuses solely on the satisfaction of the group and who values peace over conflict will create more anxiety for the congregation. Hesitant to lead strongly, the leader abdicates his or her strength to others who might not have the leader's best interests at heart. Progress occurs slowly, if at all, with this leader.[24] Either way, the congregational system, intent on maintaining homeostasis and reducing anxiety, will find ways to sabotage either of these leaders. These ministers will remain on the outskirts, unacceptable to the internal family system where true transformation can occur.

In fishing on the ocean, the pleasure of catching a big fish is unmatchable. The effort spent in reeling the weighty yellowtail snapper combined with an anticipation of eating the light, flaky meal is suddenly interrupted by a quick pull and release on the fishing line. Pulling the fish in is easy now, but the reason is clear. I've captured the head, and the happy barracuda has disappeared with my delicacy. I laugh at my loss and marvel at this beautiful creature who understands survival. This will be your life if you attempt to work in churches without a thorough understanding of family systems. But a greater danger exists if you are thrown overboard.

---

23. Friedman, *Generation to Generation*, 225–26.
24. Friedman, *Generation to Generation*, 227.

Reflection

You've been introduced to family systems in the church or religious organization. Take some time to reflect on the following:

1. What has shocked you most about people's behavior in your ministry location?

2. What images come to mind when you reflect upon the emotional balance of your current ministry setting?

3. What role do you play in this balance?

4. Who are the gatekeepers or power brokers of balance in your ministry setting? How do they keep everything balanced and in order?

5. In the story of your ministry setting, what have been its historical self-protective tendencies?

"To do God's bidding is an awesome thing. We are dealing with things that are almost impossible to handle. If the word of God does not consume us, the people of God might."[25]

25. Seymour, *Time for Healing*, 18.

Chapter 3

Man Overboard!

Then they took Jonah and threw him overboard,
and the raging sea grew calm.

—JONAH 1:15

TONY LLOYD SHARES THE story of his near drowning in a lake while swimming with a friend. He was fourteen, a self-taught swimmer, and thought he was set to race his buddy across the lake. Confidently he used the only skills he possessed to propel himself forward into the deep waters. He talks about fatigue setting in, placing him at risk, and his realization that he could not reach the shore. Listen to his moment of desperation: "I'm yelling, and I'm coughing, and the water is in my mouth . . . and all of the sudden it is completely and utterly quiet. And it occurs to me that my eyes are closed. And when I open them, there is something cold on the back of my head, and it's the mud at the bottom of the lake. And I realize that this water is dark. . . . And I'm out of air."[1] Somehow Tony finds the strength to push his body upward to the surface of the water and roll on his back while his friend guides him to the shore. Not everyone survives such an incident.

1. Lloyd, "Climate Stories," 1.

Accidental drowning is more common than one might imagine. It's the third leading cause of unintentional injury resulting in death worldwide. Over three hundred thousand annual drowning deaths occur per year according to the World Health Organization.[2] Approximately ten people a day drown and "nonfatal drowning events may occur several hundred times as frequently as reported."[3] It's difficult to know when a person is drowning. It's unlike the typical movie scene where the swimmer shouts and bobs up and down and flails their arms. Instead, it's quiet and can occur in less than a minute.[4] Due to the instinctive drowning response, the person in the water is overwhelmed and panicked, leading to rapid respirations. Much of the energy is spent on trying to breathe with little room for vocal responses. The struggling swimmer cannot call for help, sinking below the water line and rising only long enough to exhale and inhale. The arms are lateral and pressing down to leverage the body; there's no ability to raise a hand to wave for help. With the loss of normal breathing, the swimmer experiences air hunger and sinks below the water. The person will then experience hypoxemia because of either aspiration of water into the lungs or their esophagus will close creating an imbalance of carbon dioxide to oxygen. He or she will black out, relaxing the airways whereupon water enters the lungs.[5] Reading about drowning is quite different from watching it.

Early on I decided my son needed swimming lessons. Perhaps he could enjoy it as much as I did as a kid. While no ocean was near, there were plentiful lakes surrounding the area he and I could enjoy. I packed him off to the nearest swim school at a community pool. He was five years old. During the swim lesson, he and I observed a lot of commotion, screaming, and paramedics arriving on the scene. It was frightening as the lifeguard pulled a still young body out of the water. I do not know if the resuscitation efforts were successful as my son gripped me with fear and begged

2. World Health Organization, "Drowning," 1.

3. Chandy et al., "Drowning (Submersion Injuries)," 1.

4. Vittone and Pia, "It Doesn't Look Like They're Drowning," 14.

5. Fletemeyer, "What Really Happens," 1.

to leave. I could never get him in the water again. The witness to the awful event traumatized my young son.

The problem with drowning or near drowning arises from a series of mishaps that might be avoided. Jacque Wilson says, "Drowning doesn't just happen. Something precipitates drowning."[6] Children under the age of fourteen experience trouble due to poor supervision. Without proper guidance, children will go into deep water or engage in play that is dangerous. Over the age of fourteen, the American Red Cross relates accidents in the water to overconfidence, going beyond one's limits, exhaustion, disorientation, and the resulting panic.[7] Before the adult realizes they're in trouble, it's almost too late. Once in the water, the swimmer is fearful, panics, struggles, often hyperventilating, and tensing their muscles, all of which work against him or her.[8]

Many drownings might be prevented with the right education and supervision. The American Red Cross encourages families to ensure all members learn to swim and develop levels of water competency such as going into the water, breathing, staying afloat, learning to shift positions, how far is safe to swim, and getting out of the water. They encourage the use of protective barriers to prevent unsafe entries, the use of life jackets, and close supervision of children. Finally, they encourage families to be prepared in knowing what to do in case of an emergency.[9] Preparation, training, and practice can do a lot to prevent drowning.

Lack of Preparation

As you engage in church work, you may experience your best efforts prove ineffective and are unappreciated. Yet the expectations for your work remain high. While you learn to manage the various tasks of the job, nothing prepares you for the breadth and depth of

6. Wilson, "Water Safety Expert," 1.

7. Wilson, "Water Safety Expert," 1.

8. Chandy et al., "Drowning (Submersion Injuries)," 1.

9. Wilson, "Water Safety," 1.

ministry. In a survey of over eight thousand clergy, more than half stated that seminary or Bible college did not prepare them for the work.[10] Fueled by compassion and a sense of responsibility to their calling and the people, pastors experience the burden of caring for church members on a twenty-four-hour basis.[11] An enormous amount of energy is spent for others with little positive feedback for such effort and the deleterious effect of providing pastoral care is only intensified when exposed to the trauma of congregants.[12]

However, you are the first line of defense for many church members whenever a crisis occurs. Who gets the call in the middle of the night for marriage problems, serious illness, hospitalization, or death? Who makes the hospital visits, prays with the family, and helps them make funeral arrangements, performs the memorial service, all while maintaining the normal church duties? As a ministry leader, you are at the center of all life-changing events.[13] Nearly 25 percent of all Americans will seek advice from you before seeking help from a mental health professional.

During my tenure as a church starter, I recall leaving my family during a holiday meal to visit a church member who was suddenly hospitalized. As the sole chaplain for a hospital system, my family grew accustomed to waiting in the car or in my office while I responded to the latest crisis when I was called to deliver the news of an untimely death and pray with the family. I was called upon to manage people who were suicidal, psychotic, abusing drugs, and dealing with domestic violence. As interim pastor, my wife was called on Christmas Eve to provide marriage counseling to a young couple. Life brings joys but also challenges and sadness to which the church seeks your attention, comfort, blessings, and prayers. It's a constant pull that even Jesus experienced. In Mark 5, Jesus frees a man from demons, raises a little girl from the dead, and heals the woman who touches his coat. But it doesn't end there because Jesus's help is needed again. A concerned group come to

10. Krejcir, "Statistics on Pastors," 2.

11. Snelgar et al., "Preventing Compassion Fatigue," 248.

12. Snelgar et al., "Preventing Compassion Fatigue," 248.

13. Abernethy et al., "Pastors Empowerment Program," 177.

find Jesus due to the death of Jairus's daughter. Jesus goes to the synagogue leader's home and brings healing to the young girl.[14] The demands are constant because humans seek help from those who offer loving-kindness and healing. This is your role as you advise or provide spiritual guidance. Even if you do little counseling and refer those seeking help, you still serve in a gatekeeping role.[15]

Lack of Training

In a typical master's-level program for pastors, which is the gold standard of preparation for ministry, students are required to complete only one course in pastoral counseling, according to a 2014 survey of seventy seminaries.[16] While seminaries offer counseling courses, most students state they do not have time to complete the requisite ninety-hour program, work full-time, and take elective courses in counseling.[17] So leaders receive limited training in counseling during their education.[18] Most are taught to refer parishioners for therapy but there remains an issue of trust between clergy and mental health professionals. In addition, not all ministers have a thorough understanding of the services that psychologists or other mental health professionals provide.[19] Approximately 70 percent of pastors express their inability to recognize mental illness but fewer than ten percent refer to professional psychologists.[20] There is no consensus among religions or denominations about the nature of mental illness and thus no standard of care for pastors to follow.[21]

While you may choose to refuse counseling church members in favor of referring, you have a pastoral counseling role. People

14. Mark 5:35–42.
15. Baylor University, "Seminaries Do Very Little," 1.
16. Ross and Stanford, "Training and Education," 177.
17. Ross and Stanford, "Training and Education," 177.
18. Jacobson et al., "Risk for Burnout," 455–56.
19. Baylor University, "Seminaries Do Very Little," 1.
20. Farrell and Goebert, "Collaboration," 438.
21. Baylor University, "Seminaries Do Very Little," 1.

want to hear from you how to work through problems. Sometimes they are looking for affirmation or consolation. Other times, they need you to provide the biblical or spiritual foundation that seems lacking in their own lives. The function of pastoral care takes place through healing, sustaining, guiding, reconciling, and nurturing.[22] However, a lack of counseling training may prevent you from identifying the underlying reasons for spiritual distress. In a theology class, I asked students how to handle a person with depression. Most of them responded that they would advise, encourage, and share scriptures of hope. Certainly, these are necessary things, but I reminded the class that the cause of the depression indicates the type of help needed. If a person has an autoimmune disorder, Scripture will help, but they might need a medical exam and an appropriate medication to address the physiological cause. However, if the depression occurs in a cycle where the individual experiences high periods with delusional episodes followed by depression, then a psychiatric evaluation is necessary. The person may have bipolar disorder. Perhaps the person is depressed, and it's a side effect of a certain medication. If it's related to a recent loss, as in bereavement, then support, encouragement, Scripture, and prayer will be helpful. There is always time for prayer and healing. However, there's a lot more assessment of individual issues that needs to occur, and more than you may have either the time or training. As a recent graduate in the field of counseling said, "I had no idea how complex counseling was until I started doing it every day. It can actually be overwhelming." Primarily, you need training in assessment and referral, and in prevention of burnout and compassion fatigue.

Exposure Risk

While counseling people can be satisfying, it also places you at an increased risk for burnout and compassion fatigue.[23] Left un-

---

22. Scots College, "Five Crucial Functions," 1.
23. Snelgar et al., "Preventing Compassion Fatigue," 248.

treated, you will soon experience increasing levels of anxiety and depression. The standard advice for burnout prevention is living a balanced life, healthy habits in nutrition and exercise, taking time off, and having a social network. While these are useful suggestions, they will not prevent burnout or compassion fatigue. For many clergy, these recommendations make the wrong assumptions about the causes and leave ministers feeling guilty when they cannot follow the advice.[24] There is little recognition that systems cause burnout. "People burn out because they work in systems that burn them out. The problem is external: too much work, too little support, rigid work schedules, difficult parishioners, being 'on call' twenty-four hours a day, seven days a week, excessive bureaucracy, unhelpful and often irrelevant denominational structures."[25]

While the cause of burnout is often related to poorly designed structures of care, compassion fatigue occurs because of the minister's exposure to the crisis and trauma of their people. Here is Bob Field's story:

> I was thinking about everything I needed to get done, and the mountain of other people's brokenness and needs. I wanted people to be released to live transformed lives. . . . Trying to authentically engage with those who lose loved ones, those whose relationships are falling apart, those being persecuted, those who are angry, those who are depressed, those who are disappointed in life, those who express freely the inadequacies of the church . . . and the list goes on. I think deep down I knew a crash was coming.[26]

The experience of burnout and compassion fatigue resemble that of the person who is drowning. Overconfidence leads ministers to providing care for the suffering for which they are ill prepared and often leads to emotional exhaustion. Pastors often perceive their responsibility is to continue assisting others while

---

24. Grosch and Olsen, "Clergy Burnout," 620.
25. Grosch and Olsen, "Clergy Burnout," 620.
26. Field, "Falling Apart," 11.

trying to draw strength from their spiritual resources.[27] After all, that is what they teach their parishioners to do. Meanwhile, they cannot "catch their breath," are swimming in waters beyond their level of competency, and reticent to ask for the help they need. That's why some ministers describe their experience as "drowning for Jesus." Their calling to serve God feels like they must sacrifice their emotional health for the sake of God's children. In a 2007 study of over a thousand pastors, 100 percent of the responding ministers stated they knew of a colleague who had burnout or compassion fatigue, and almost all reported they were worn out.[28] Yet clergy are reluctant to disclose such struggles.[29] Faced with a role that requires self-containment to lead congregants, pastors experience an imbalance in relationship connection,[30] leaving them to sink below the surface while grasping for air.

Without an adequate understanding of the causes of burnout and compassion fatigue, and the tendency to provide short-sighted solutions, you are unlikely to receive the help you most need. It is important to explain, educate, and introduce the life-saving measures. Similar to the American Red Cross recommendations, you and your family need lessons in swimming the ministerial waters including competency development, protective barriers, and supervision. Providing such education will ensure safe swimming instead of sinking when thrown overboard.

Reflection

Think about your ministry and the following questions:

1. What elements in your ministry system contribute to your feelings of being overwhelmed?

2. Of the three risks mentioned, lack of preparation, lack of training, and exposure, which are your greatest risks?

27. Snelgar et al., "Preventing Compassion Fatigue," 247.
28. Snelgar et al., "Preventing Compassion Fatigue," 248.
29. Bettis, "4 Great Challenges," 1.
30. Salwen et al., "Self-Disclosure," 506.

3. What were the most rewarding and challenging aspects of your preparation for ministry?

4. What and/or who have you sacrificed in your practice of ministry?

5. What aspects of your practice leave you feeling like you are drowning?

6. Since clergy are often the first support professionals consulted for a wide range of issues, what does this say about your vocation?

7. What are the strengths and limitations of this dynamic?

"When ministry is under siege, things are not always as they seem. When ministry is under siege, the potential to misread God's intent is probably never greater."[31]

31. Allen, *Before You Quit*, 42.

Chapter 4

Sink or Swim

The engulfing waters threatened me, the deep surrounded me;
seaweed was wrapped around my head.

—JONAH 2:5

DRIVING TO WORK TOOK twenty minutes but felt like an eternity.
The closer I drew, the faster my heart pounded. I tried to ignore it
but then my stomach churned, and my head spun. "It's okay. You
can do this. You do this every day. You're good at this." It was as if
I were trying to convince myself that I was good enough. By the
time I walked into my beautiful office, surrounded by windows
with a view of a well-manicured lawn and plenty of flowers, I could
not enjoy the moment. This was my time. I had my dream job and
was fulfilling my calling from God. I was well known and was ap-
proaching the prime of my career. I had the best team in town. It
couldn't have been any better. But I was burning out.

A few years later, Jerry called and said,

> I don't know what to do. I can't think. I can't sleep. When
> I do sleep, I dream about them. I can't stop thinking
> about my church people, especially the ones who share
> their stories of woundedness. I get irritated with them

and find my caustic humor is hurting them. I don't know
if I can continue doing this. But what else can I do? I
spent a lot of time and money to become a pastor and it's
eating my lunch.

Affirming Jerry's decision to be vulnerable, I shared my story
with him. It was important for him to know he was not alone; he
is an excellent minister and recovery was a step away. My job was
to honor him and his professionalism while providing him with a
sense of hope. And it was important for Jerry to name this problem. Jerry said, "I think I have compassion fatigue. Now tell me
what I need to do."

Your job is dependent on being an emotionally healthy individual. Churches expect that you set an example for parishioners.
So, you harbor the secret within, knowing you are swimming in
waters over your head. Working with people makes you suscep-
tible to burnout or compassion fatigue. There is growing concern,
emphasis, and research to guide you through prevention and treatment once you openly identify and acknowledge the struggle.

There are some who declare burnout is a separate and unique
experience from compassion fatigue while others view them as the
same. Leading researchers in the field of burnout conceptualize it
as a syndrome wherein three primary processes occur: emotional
exhaustion, cynicism (leading to disengagement), and a sense of
inefficacy.[1] In other words, your internal resources are depleted,
your perspective or view of the situation or people are tainted, and
you feel as though your efforts no longer matter. Most pastors express it in the following ways: "I feel drained by my ministry role."
"I have this continuous sense of sadness." "I feel discouraged in
my work."[2] Other ministers report self-doubt and feelings of inadequacy.[3] It is the feeling and fatigue arising from these that leads
you to say, "I'll just do less. I'll set more boundaries. I'll learn to say
no. I'll just quit."

---

1. Maslach and Leiter, "Understanding the Burnout Experience," 103.
2. Francis et al., "Work-Related Psychological Wellbeing," 3.
3. Barnard and Curry, "Relationship of Clergy Burnout," 150.

While Freudenberger[4] first conceptualized burnout in the 1970s, it was Carla Joinson who coined the term compassion fatigue when talking of what nurses experience.[5] Shortly thereafter, Charles Figley began using the term to refer to those traumatized by hearing the trauma stories of those whom they served.[6] While Joinson and her colleagues were describing the burnout symptoms of nurses, the field of traumatology was describing the experience of first responders. Both used the same term, compassion fatigue, to explain the phenomenon experienced by professionals. However, Charles Figley and his colleagues viewed the experience as a result of secondary traumatization, in other words, the result of hearing or seeing the trauma of others. Sorenson and his colleagues in reviewing more than three hundred journal articles stated,

> Compassion fatigue is often conflated with burnout, secondary traumatic stress, and compassion stress. While the terms are used interchangeably in the literature, it is unclear whether they are in fact synonymous. Some of this overlap occurred due to the evolution of the concept of compassion fatigue. . . . Some led to Figley's further research and conceptualization of secondary traumatic stress to explain the costs of caring many supportive parties experienced when they learned of someone else's trauma.[7]

A third view of compassion fatigue, offered by Miller and Sprang, is that the occurring job stress is related to a lack of self-regulation during a counseling session. In other words, rather than "caring too much," the inability to tolerate intense experiences, and the subsequent withdrawal of engagement from the person who shares, lies at the heart of the symptoms.[8] Certainly ministers face intense situations that are uncomfortable.

4. Freudenberger and Richelson, *Burn-Out*, 11–13.

5. Joinson, "Coping," 117–18.

6. Figley, *Compassion Fatigue*, 5.

7. Sorenson et al., "Understanding Compassion Fatigue," 456–57.

8. Miller and Sprang, "Components-Based Practice," 153.

The minister faces both unwieldy expectations and exposure to trauma material in pastoral care.

> Compassion fatigue can therefore be understood as a re-action to overexposure to human suffering which mani-fests in feelings of burnout, secondary traumatic stress, and depersonalization from one's job. When pastors experience severe compassion fatigue and its resultant spiritual, emotional, mental, and physical consequences, then they run the risk of failing their churches and con-gregations through the conflict, destruction, and chaos that may arise.[9]

While compassion fatigue and burnout have similar symp-toms, they are unique in some ways. Compassion fatigue is acute and often mimics post-traumatic stress disorder in its physical hyperarousal and avoidance symptoms.[10] The pastor with compas-sion fatigue, like Jerry, will have thoughts about people or inci-dences that disrupt activities, possibly reoccurring dreams, which cause a sense of urgency, or an increase in blood pressure or heart rate, resulting in avoidance of the people involved or the subject matter. My experience is indicative of burnout, especially the neg-ative thoughts about my professional performance and feelings of inadequacy. Louw explains,

> It is indeed very difficult to differentiate between com-passion fatigue and burnout. The two are interrelated to the same phenomenon of exhaustion and over-exposure. Both refer to action and attitude. The cause of burnout is accumulative stress, with the tendency to withdraw and to avoid being exposed. Compassion fatigue is the result of excessive over-identification and constant exposure to severe forms of human suffering.[11]

The nature of pastoral work includes the offer of a compassion-ate presence. This requires emotional intelligence, empathy, accurate listening skills, and acknowledgment of another person's narrative.

9. Snelgar et al., "Preventing Compassion Fatigue," 248.

10. Sorenson et al., "Understanding Compassion Fatigue," 457.

11. Louw, "Compassion Fatigue," 2.

It means portraying to the one who shares that you bear witness to their suffering, both as a human and as an extension of God.

> Being "moved" by the Other's experience involves proximate action. That is, in being moved I communicate to the Other that I am with them in their suffering. Compassion without proximate solidarity is mere pity . . . [true] compassion necessarily depends on humility and courage; the humility to accept the limitations of our truth and the courage to acknowledge and contain the anxiety that accompanies existential uncertainty and ambiguity, which together fosters hospitality toward the Other.[12]

There are times when you will become weary of facing conflict, injustice, oppression, fear, anxiety, and hatred while offering hope, direction, faithfulness, and unending inspiration. Amid the demands, you are called to focus on existential life questions, helping parishioners to connect tragedy and theology, the consequence of sin and God's redemptive plan, and the acceptance of human limitation with Christ's call to follow.[13] It's a wonder you can continue to function with all of these requisites.

However, it's important to recognize that while you may have burnout or compassion fatigue, you can be highly satisfied with the job. How is that possible? To answer this question, Leslie Francis developed the Francis Burnout Inventory to measure both burnout or compassion fatigue and ministry satisfaction. He developed the balanced affect model, inferring that the positive effects of ministry balance the negative circumstances. They are not opposite ends of the spectrum but rather two different phenomena that pastors experience.[14] In Randall's work with clergy, seven out of ten reported their ministry having a positive influence on others and over 60 percent reported satisfaction from working with people and were glad they entered the ministry.[15] Yet these same ministers were reporting burnout or compassion fatigue. Clearly the level

12. LaMothe, "Broken and Empty," 461–63.

13. Louw, "Compassion Fatigue," 3.

14. Francis et al., "Work-Related Psychological Wellbeing," 2.

15. Randall, "Clergy Burnout," 338.

of satisfaction in ministry is providing these pastors with enough fulfillment to continue serving despite the emotional exhaustion.[16]

Elijah's story bears witness to the experience of both a successful ministry and burnout. On Mount Carmel, Elijah demonstrates God's power over Baal.[17] This was a highlight in his career, and many of the people cry out for God after the magnificent display. Yet when Jezebel threatens Elijah, he runs away in fear of his life. He reaches a point in the desert where he is exhausted, discouraged, disillusioned, feeling failure, a sense of abandonment, and where he prays for his own death. He needs nourishment, retreat, self-examination, worship, and a renewal of his call. He falls asleep under the broom tree and is awakened by a heavenly being to eat and then rest some more. Awakened again he responds to God's angel to eat in preparation for a journey.[18] It appears Elijah has lost his way. The disorientation he experiences is a barrier to his continuing ministry. This is how some pastors describe burnout, and with it comes a sense of frustration and hopelessness.

I was driving home one night when a sudden snowstorm hit. Within a few minutes, the storm was a whiteout and visibility reduced to a few feet. I could not see where I was going or even where I had been. Although the road was familiar, I was disoriented and wondered if I was lost. I thought, "Did I make the wrong turn somewhere? Where does this road end? Am I on the wrong side of the road?" My anxiety continued to rise. I thought about stopping, but that seemed as dangerous as moving forward. Turning around was no better. The only thing I knew to do was keep moving forward. Slowly I drove ahead, reassuring myself that I knew this road and it would guide me safely to a place where I could see. Eventually I arrived at a recognizable place. Although the confusion was unnerving, I was safe all along.[19]

There are times in ministry when you will find yourself in the midst of a tempest and unable to see anything. It is disquieting

16. Randall, "Clergy Burnout," 338.

17. 1 Kgs 18.

18. 1 Kgs 18:4–8.

19. Hoppe, "Self-Directed Approach," 143.

and doubt sinks in as you struggle to swim against the tide. As the bewilderment arrives, it becomes like seaweed wrapping around your throat. You may think you have lost your way. Did you misunderstand God's call? Make a wrong turn? You want to get away from the undercurrent, but the harder you try, the further you sink. Caught in the middle of burnout or compassion fatigue, you need an escape plan. The right skills with the right equipment at a difficult time will save you.

Reflection

There are times in ministry when you're lost in the storm and unable to see clearly. It is unsettling and brings doubts with it. Did you miss a signpost? Make a wrong turn? These times may be disorienting. Take a moment to complete the following checklist:

- There are times when I wonder why I chose the ministry.
- Sometimes I wonder if I made a mistake in coming to this church.
- I wonder if God is pleased with what I'm doing in my ministry.
- It is difficult to please the people in this church.
- Sometimes my work is filled with trivial things that are unfulfilling.[20]

Now take a moment to reflect on the following questions:

1. What have been my greatest disappointments in ministry?

2. What do I worry about most frequently?

3. What is my greatest fear?

"Take heed to yourselves lest you perish while you call upon others to heed of perishing, and lest you famish yourselves while you prepare their food."[21]

20. Hoppe, "Self-Directed Approach," 143.
21. Baxter, *Reformed Pastor*, 2.

Part II

Finding Your Stroke

Then the word of the Lord came to Jonah a second time: "Go to the great city of Nineveh and proclaim to it the message I give you."

—JONAH 3:1

WHEN GOD CALLS YOU to serve, it comes with the promise of empowerment. To each objection Moses raises, God responds: "I will be with you."[1] In Jeremiah's hesitation, God says, "I have put my words in your mouth."[2] William Hulme emphasized that attunement with God brings the "eye of faith."[3] Yet imagine the person who sacrifices his or her personal pursuits to fulfill this calling and then faces a failure of vision. What happened? Where is this power? Why are marvelous things not happening if God is leading the way?

Dallas and his wife, Susan, come to my office seeking help. He is not excited about the visit, but Susan insists. Married for ten years, Susan says she is at her wit's end. They married when Dallas was starting a church and it seemed so exciting. The church had a strong start in the fastest growing city in the state. However,

1. Exod 3:15.
2. Jer 1:9.
3. Hulme, *Managing Stress*, 57.

the growth of the church did not match the growth of the surrounding area. The church grew slowly, and Dallas was reticent to release control of the church to rely upon lay leaders, leaving himself responsible for most things. Susan said, "I don't really have a husband. I'm married to a church and it never ceases." Dallas has stopped talking with Susan about his worries because he doesn't want to burden her with church issues. Dallas's eyes are full of concern and yet he has little support. The church is not connected to a denomination and Dallas never identified a support group or mentor. He's doing this alone. This is not what he expected when he heard God tell him to start this church. Dallas denies any symptoms of burnout or compassion fatigue, but he is at risk of those. Now is the time to prevent either from occurring.

Many people believe the right way to prevent or treat burnout or compassion fatigue is to stop doing so much. People attribute the stress disorder to being too busy, or being over-committed, or working too many hours. Look around though. Some of the busiest ministry leaders are doing fine. What's the difference? People have identified the wrong element as the cause, and therefore the solutions fall short. Doing less does not reinvigorate you. Instead, it raises your sense of inefficacy and creates more doubt. Setting more boundaries, while healthy, possibly alienates you, creating distance and isolation. That disengagement increases your cynicism and reinforces your view of the world, or people, as things that invade your personal space. Requests become intruders to which you feel resentment, leading to further exhaustion and a loss of personal accomplishment.

Many will say the key to avoiding burnout or compassion fatigue is self-care. They will tell Pastor Dallas: "Just take some time off." "You need to eat healthier." "Get some exercise." (Pastor Dallas does those things.) While all of those suggestions are healthy things for you to do, they don't prevent burnout either. There is little correlation between poor self-care and burnout, and even less relationship to compassion fatigue. David von Schlichten says,

> If the general population and even experts are mistakenly thinking that clergy burnout and poor self-care are

necessarily bound together, then the assumption may be that better self-care will result in reduced burnout. However, as I have seen in some of the research, there is not always a close correlation between poor self-care and burnout. Thus, reducing burnout is not as simple as encouraging clergy to engage in better self-care.[4]

Instead, the advice for self-care may be more harmful for some, according to Maslach, because of the stigmatization of burnout as a sign of weakness or incompetence.[5] While self-care is certainly a component of prevention, there are other salient factors that prevent burnout or compassion fatigue. When people suggest that clergy increase self-care, sometimes this is the message the pastor hears, "If you are experiencing burnout, it is your own fault, and you are the only one who can do something about it."[6] This assumption contributes to the increasing loneliness ministers experience by assigning both guilt and responsibility for recovery to them. This characterization prevents ministers from taking helpful actions to prevent burnout. Likewise, the general advice to prevent compassion fatigue is to stop counseling parishioners. That becomes an impossible task when ministers are the first people with whom a church member connects amid crisis.[7]

Understanding the causes of burnout and compassion fatigue helps with outlining preventive techniques. The leading researcher in burnout, Christina Maslach, suggests prevention is a far better strategy than waiting to treat burnout after it becomes a problem. She encourages implementing steps that reduce the risks as a primary strategy.[8] In the past forty years, researchers have worked to determine why people experience work-related stress disorders such as burnout and compassion fatigue. When burnout was conceived, the focus was on personality and traits unique to an individual that create burnout. Internal factors cause the

4. Von Schlichten, "Pastoral Mystique," 194.
5. Maslach, "Finding Solutions," 146.
6. Maslach, "Finding Solutions," 146.
7. Hendron et al., "Unseen Cost," 227.
8. Maslach, "Finding Solutions," 147.

syndrome.[9] However, further investigation reveals that organizational dynamics are also responsible. These variables are the focus of this section and suggestions on how to "fix the person" and "fix the job."[10] But those alone are insufficient to prevent burnout.[11]

So, what's the right antidote? Engagement. While counterintuitive, getting more involved may be the answer you are seeking. Engagement can be positive and fulfilling. It comes from your sense of calling or belief that even the most minute changes matter. Rather than distancing yourself from a situation or parishioner or activities, diving in deeper to understand the universal elements of the dilemma can invigorate and increase inspiration and pride. Simply put, engagement increases satisfaction.[12] You do not burn out or experience compassion fatigue because of over-involvement or caring too much. Actually, higher levels of empathy are protective.[13] Being properly engaged means that you focus on the meaning and purpose of your work, noticing how you view it and how you experience other people. It means controlling your thoughts about a situation or person or church, reducing that negativity to manageable levels.[14]

Healthy engagement involves revisiting the story of your calling, the situation, the church, the people, or your efficacy until you capture the positive mission involved. You find the meaning of suffering and then move to trust that what you're doing serves a greater purpose and creates a transformation that is larger than one person's job. That's what Jonah didn't capture. He could not accept the positive outcome of the nation turning to God in repentance. He was focused on being punitive. None of us know Jonah's ending story because the book ends abruptly. Does he find his way through his resistance to rewrite his own story?

9. Maslach and Leiter, "Understanding the Burnout Experience," 105.

10. Maslach, "Finding Solutions," 147.

11. Maslach, "Finding Solutions," 146.

12. Upadyaya et al., "From Job Demands," 106.

13. Miller and Sprang, "Components-Based Practice," 155.

14. Miller and Sprang, "Components-Based Practice," 157–58.

Examining and renewing your calling is akin to wearing a life preserver. It keeps you alive and afloat while searching for help and direction. With experience you learn to wear the life-saving device at all times, a constant reminder that God undergirds the call to minister to a hurting world and that you are never alone in this. Swimming the ocean requires balancing and resiliency. You must find your life-sustaining stroke and know how to navigate the swells and rises of the water.

Chapter 5

Charting the Waters

Jonah obeyed the word of the Lord and went to Nineveh.

—JONAH 3:3A

IN HIGH SCHOOL, I joined the swim team. I didn't know it then, and although I had excellent swimming skills, I could never be an elite athlete in the sport. I am not built to succeed in competition. Look at any Olympian swimmer and you'll notice their similarities. Performance swimmers are tall. The average height of the 2016 Olympic finalist male swimmers in Rio de Janeiro was six foot two inches, which is taller than the average male.[1] You also see that they have longer arms and torsos. In fact, the science of anthropometry considers the relationship of body weight, height, muscle circumference, and distribution of body fat and skeletal muscle mass.[2] Olympic scouts watch pediatric swimmers to identify young talent to send to development programs. The perfect swimmer will have certain characteristics that create a high anthropometry score; longer arms in relation to height, longer torso with shorter, muscular

---

1. Mortenson, "What Makes the Perfect Swimmer's Body?," 1.

2. Bond et al., "Association between Anthropometric Variables," 2.

legs, and large hands.[3] These features allow the swimmer to reach farther, pulling more water with every stroke, with powerful legs for propulsion but that don't create a lot of drag. In addition, swimmers with large hands, feet, and lungs can use their extremities as paddles and fins while the large lungs increase buoyancy and endurance.[4] Flexibility is also key, especially in the shoulders to lengthen strokes and in the ankles to increase the surface area of the foot, pushing more water backwards.[5] My height was average with average arms. The only real advantage I had was flexibility, a little double jointed, which was great for entertainment at social gatherings, but otherwise not very useful. My body isn't designed to succeed in Olympic swimming, so I didn't pursue it. Swimming is a sport that's highly individual, unlike football.

In football, the coach can place a large athlete as a guard. He may be slower, but he will prevent any player from breaking through. You probably don't want to use him as a kicker if he can't kick well. Players' weaknesses and strengths can be assessed, and a player placed where he or she functions best. Or consider the sport of soccer, which my sons played. My oldest son was quick, aggressive, and had good endurance, so placing him as a defender made good sense. He could run all over the field quickly and never run out of energy. But my younger son, full of personality with a sharp eye, made a great goalie. He could taunt and tease the opponents into attempting goals yet was ever ready to block whatever came his way. It also helped that he had large hands to catch the ball. Placing people in the right position requires an understanding of the interplay between fit of personality, aptitude, and skill. This is an important yet underemphasized task in ministry career development. It means understanding yourself accurately, strengthening your current skills, and finding the right fit of job for you.

Success in ministry occurs through planning. No one sets out to sea without charting the course first and identifying the troublesome areas. Identifiable risks for burnout and compassion fatigue

3. Mortenson, "What Makes the Perfect Swimmer's Body?," 1.
4. Mortenson, "What Makes the Perfect Swimmer's Body?," 1.
5. Mortenson, "What Makes the Perfect Swimmer's Body?," 1.

should be addressed at the beginning of your ministry career. The factors that cause the most vulnerability include being new to ministry, a mismatch between you and an organization or church, your personality tendencies, your exposure to trauma, and inadequate spiritual self-care. If you adopt strategies to enhance or balance these risks, then your susceptibility to burnout or compassion fatigue can decrease. Interestingly, the preventive measures have less to do with rest and physical activity than you might imagine.

Risk One: Novices

The first way clergy are at risk for burnout and compassion fatigue occurs when entering the field as they adjust to ministry expectations.[6] Mentoring and coaching are necessary for the novice. All people new to ministry ought to seek an experienced mentor to guide, if not coach or supervise them. On an organizational or denominational level, administrators can help new ministers succeed by offering support individually and in groups. However, it is also important that organizations openly discuss the risks for burnout and compassion fatigue with ministers and working on ways to destigmatize the stress-related syndromes, so ministers feel safe to express difficulties without fear of blame or the thought someone will pathologize their experience.

Our entry into ministry full-time occurred when we were sent to start a church. We had no experience in church planting, but we were willing to accept the low annual salary of twelve thousand dollars. Expecting our first child, our eyes were full of wonder and great expectation. We believed that God would work the miracles needed to turn a small group of people into a growing congregation. We did not expect the difficulties. We were introverted people trying to do the extroverted job of drawing people into an evangelical church. We spent five years working diligently to build something that would last. Sinking to a new low, we realized this was not a good ministry choice for either of us, deciding

6. Doolittle, "Burnout and Coping," 36.

to leave. The church is still there and is a small but strong church. It took many years to realize that we did something good there, but at the time we felt like we were failing. We needed a mentor to help us through that difficult time.

Risk Two: Mismatch of Person and Job

A second risk factor is the mismatch between you and a church or other organization. There are some workplaces that create an environment that places employees at risk for burnout. Those churches or religious organizations that demand too many hours, or do not provide adequate resources for the job, or do not allow for autonomy will be detrimental to you. Likewise, those situations where you have little control over decision-making, especially regarding your job, do not receive timely rewards, either monetary, related to benefits, or positive feedback, or treat you unfairly will cause burnout.[7] Sometimes your ideas or dreams are dissimilar to the organization's vision or values. Add to these factors, small congregations and churches with high stress and conflict and you are at a high risk of burnout.[8]

Sometimes, groups can work to create an environment that supports the church mission and provides you with an adequate workload, plentiful resources, autonomy, decision-making power, while offering constructive feedback and affirmation, and fairness. When churches or organizations work hard to provide these, they can then possibly attract ministers who stay longer, which helps stabilize the church and position it for growth. Being wise, you must have this discussion prior to accepting a call. In this way, you are aware beforehand of any conditions that will not work for you.

While you can hardly "prevent" the experience of smaller churches or disagreements in such churches, you can use the mentoring process and the denominational support to prepare for managing these situations. This is when collaboration with others

7. Maslach, "Finding Solutions," 149–50.
8. Doolittle, "Burnout and Coping," 36.

becomes key and there may be times when someone steps in to mediate difficult circumstances. The best scenario is preparation and coaching for you.

Jonathan had no idea what was happening when he was called into the board meeting. Fresh from seminary, he wanted to make a difference. He'd served time in the military, finished graduate school, and was certain he could master the art of pastoring a church. However, he did not know this church had fired the previous two ministers, and that there was a long history of conflict in this small church. He was drawn into a battle for which he was unprepared. He was fired in that board meeting. It was a few months later before he learned of the other pastors who were asked to leave. He thought of leaving the ministry but sought direction by entering a clinical pastoral education program. "That saved my life," Jonathan said. Today Jonathan has completed many years of ministry service as a pastor and chaplain.

Risk Three: Personality

A third risk factor is unhealthy coping mechanisms,[9] and poor emotional resilience, or low emotional stability.[10] Certain qualities and characteristics, even in ministry settings, make for a good fit of person to job. Without the right traits, you are at greater risk of developing burnout. While there are many types of personality assessments or inventories, the most notable and researched formulation is the Five Factor Model of Personality.[11] This model is the most widely used in burnout research and views personality on five dimensions: openness, conscientiousness, extraversion, agreeableness, and emotional stability (formerly called neuroticism).[12] I offer a brief description of each.

9. Visker et al., "Ministry-Related Burnout," 952.
10. Alessandri et al., "Job Burnout," 827.
11. Alarcon et al., "Relationships," 246.
12. Alarcon et al., "Relationships," 246.

Openness refers to the person accepting of novel experiences, and those who are creative and intelligent individuals.[13] People with openness adopt a curious stance toward stress events which allows them to problem solve with ingenuity.[14] It makes good sense that the clergy person high in openness is less likely to experience emotional exhaustion, unless that openness leads to unnecessary and multiple risks. If the pastor engages in too many risky behaviors, then the likelihood of emotional exhaustion increases.[15] Conscientiousness refers to the drive to accomplish.[16] This quality is often found in ministers who are self-disciplined, systematic, and steady. What is interesting are those people who state that the "A-type" person, or those driven to succeed, who set more goals and become busy, are likely to get "burned out." There's no evidence that an achiever is more likely to burn out than anyone else.

The next broad characteristic is extraversion, or those individuals who are confident, active, and seek excitement. The extroverting minister is less likely to experience burnout as compared to the introverting clergy who seeks isolation.[17] The extrovert is more optimistic, seeks help when needed, and enjoys a large social network from which he or she can gain support or strength. Agreeableness is the quality concerned with interpersonal relationships, cooperation, caring, trust, and sympathy toward others.[18] Because of the emphasis upon relationship to others, a person high in agreeableness possibly experiences a higher level of emotional exhaustion over time. This may be due to the unselfish, caring nature of the person high in agreeableness. However, it can also serve as a protective factor for the minister and is positively associated with a personal sense of accomplishment.[19]

---

13. Alessandri et al., "Job Burnout," 828.

14. Sharma and Kashyap, "Influence of the Big Five," 18.

15. Sharma and Kashyap, "Influence of the Big Five," 18.

16. Alessandri et al., "Job Burnout," 828.

17. Visker et al., "Ministry-Related Burnout," 952.

18. Alarcon et al., "Relationships," 247.

19. Alessandri et al., "Job Burnout," 825.

Emotional stability refers to freedom from negative emotions such as anxiety, fearfulness, irritability, and general discontentment. It is the most important personality trait that predicts risk for burnout.[20] Those ministry leaders with lower emotional stability may have an increased concern or desire to please others and a sense of shame if that does not happen. The result is increased anger and depression.[21] People with low emotional stability have more difficulty coping with negative emotions and are more vulnerable to stress. They may use ineffective coping mechanisms such as self-criticism, wishful thinking, and denial.[22]

It's important to note that while personality traits change little during a lifetime, the ability to develop self-efficacy has the potential to increase, influencing the degree to which you experience emotional instability. Self-efficacy arises out of your internal beliefs and is amenable to change with the help of coaching or therapy. Higher self-efficacy induces positive perceptions and changes the degree to which you control your life.[23] When you focus on increasing your resiliency skills, then general well-being and authenticity increase, leading to a sense of thriving.[24] Resiliency occurs through self-awareness, self-reflectivity, and self-control.[25]

Risk Four: Exposure to Trauma

While the previous risks discussed may lead to burnout, there are additional risks for you that may increase the possibility of compassion fatigue. This is where it's important to understand the differences between burnout and compassion fatigue. The primary difference is the exposure to traumatic events or hearing

---

20. Alessandri et al., "Job Burnout," 825.

21. Barnard and Curry, "Relationship of Clergy Burnout," 4.

22. Alessandri et al., "Job Burnout," 825.

23. Alessandri et al., "Job Burnout," 827–42.

24. Bloom, *Flourishing*, 2.

25. Bloom, *Flourishing*, 2.

the suffering stories from a congregant's life that lie at the heart of compassion fatigue.

Your job involves multiple roles, including the provision of care and concern, offering hope and reconciliation. Most of this occurs throughout the week as parishioners seek ministry help. The stories of suffering overwhelm you at times. There are few other occupations that are inclined or expected to listen to these narratives as the pastor. Imagine the stories and the questions. "Pastor, why did God take my twenty-year-old son in a car accident but not my ninety-year-old mother with dementia who has no quality of life?" How do you respond to this? Or, how about this question, "Reverend Smith, why did my father sexually abuse me when I was a little girl? I can't call God 'father' because that triggers such awful memories." Or when you sit with your lead deacon and the deacon's spouse, learning the couple is on the verge of divorce, and the deacon, your favorite one, by the way, is abusing alcohol and watching pornography? For all of these, you may suffer from the pain related to the deep compassion you feel toward all church members. How can you deal with this overload?

Constantly confronted with people in need, you may feel satisfied and yet emotionally exhausted. If you are unable or unwilling to set and maintain healthy boundaries and continue to "pour yourself out," you will soon experience the accompanying depersonalization and inefficacy indicative of burnout.[26] The protective factor is the degree to which you practice self-compassion, meaning kindness toward yourself during stress, and the ability to refrain from negative and repetitive thinking, or rumination, when setting limits.[27]

Upon hearing the events surrounding 9/11, Roger knew he needed to act quickly. After receiving the blessing from his congregation, he packed up and spent the next few months in New York City working with people affected. On one of his visits to return home, he shared part of the stories and devastation with us. His eyes filled with tears, and he shook his head, saying, "It's really too

26. Doolittle, "Burnout and Coping," 37.
27. Barnard and Curry, "Relationship of Clergy Burnout," 12.

terrible to describe it all. I don't know if I'll ever be free of what I saw and heard." Roger willingly placed himself at risk when exposing himself to the trauma. He doesn't regret it, but it changed him forever. Within a month after working as a 9/11 responder, Roger noted his compassion fatigue. He couldn't get certain images out of his mind, and he continued to hear the voices of victims as they recalled their stories, and he felt as if he had been present on that day, but he wasn't. Roger was having trouble sleeping and difficulty concentrating. He couldn't seem to return to "normal." He came seeking help.

In our time together, Roger described his life history. Part of that included an event that changed his life and career. He was an all-state football player and was being scouted by prestigious football programs. But in his junior year, Roger was sacked by another player, and in the process broke his leg and tore several tendons. He was out for the rest of the season recuperating from several surgeries. When he recovered, he couldn't gain the speed or accuracy he once possessed. He played his senior year, but none of the recruiters retained interest in him. He played some college ball but it was never the same and so he dropped out in his sophomore year in college. It was a traumatic loss of identity and career. He never grieved that loss and so when he responded to the 9/11 crisis, he had little awareness how hearing the loss of family, friends, and career paths would trigger his own sense of loss. Roger had a primary traumatic experience that was unresolved. In our time together, he learned how that placed him at risk of further traumatization, which was occurring when he attempted to help others. Once he dealt with the primary trauma successfully, his symptoms decreased, and he could continue his successful ministry.

Risk Five: Inadequate Self-Care

Yes, this is it. You've been looking for this section, haven't you? By all means, if you do not care for yourself in substantive ways, you are at risk for burnout or compassion fatigue. But what does this mean? What types of unhealthy habits place you at risk? The lack of care for mental health issues such as anxiety or depression increase your risk, and a limited support network, a lack of self-awareness or the inability to monitor your physical and emotional reactions to stress, and the negative cognitions and stories you tell yourself about the situation, the event, the people, or yourself.[28] You thought I would say not taking care of your body, right? Certainly, healthy nutrition, exercise, and relaxation contribute to your overall sense of well-being, as it does for all of us.[29] However, not doing those things does not place you at higher risk for burn-out or compassion fatigue. There is one other risk factor though, and it is the lack of using spiritual resources.

Your spiritual life is vital. Having a clear sense of calling and a secure attachment to God prepares you for the difficulties that arise. It is imperative you cultivate a relationship that provides a sound foundation and produces the resources to maintain spiritual growth.[30] If you have difficulty tolerating intense conversations, and the subsequent theological confusion, then you may also experience burnout or compassion fatigue. Louw explains it this way,

> Compassion fatigue is closely related to the trauma of overexposure. However, it cuts deeper. It is fundamentally about the illness or spiritual pathology of "professional disempowerment." It is a condition related to the sickness of professional helplessness, and the fear not to be able to deal furthermore with human suffering in a sustainable way; it describes more or less a condition of habitual incompetence . . . it does not primarily reside in a lack of skills, but in a lack of resilience within the face of the desperate situation of human beings and the predicament of an overwhelming sense of failure and vulnerability.[31]

The fatigue you experience includes the disillusionment of your theological foundation and demands a reexamination of your spiritual faith. Louw considers compassion fatigue as a "yearning

28. Jacobson et al., "Risk for Burnout," 462–63.
29. Bloom, "Flourishing," 14.
30. Bickerton et al., "Well-Being," 10.
31. Louw, "Compassion Fatigue," 4.

for wholeness" in which only a deepening relationship with God can heal.[32] It means developing a new religious coping style, one that is collaborative, sharing responsibility with God for solving the problems, instead of trying to resolve them on your own.[33] It means rethinking the relationship you have with God. It relies upon maintaining your spiritual compass and knowing where true north lies. That prevents you from getting lost at sea.

Reflection

This chapter speaks of the risks of burnout. Which of these risks fit you?

- I've been in ministry for five years or less.

- My current ministry setting or current position does not fit my personality.

- My vision and my organization's vision are too different.

- I work in a small congregation or in an environment with high conflict.

- I struggle with anxiety and self-esteem.

- I have experienced trauma in my past, either in childhood, or during a work experience. Or I have been exposed to the trauma of someone else.

- I neglect to care for myself, often letting the needs of others outweigh my personal needs.

What do your responses tell you? In what way do these factors contribute to your risk for burnout or compassion fatigue?

"Ordination to the Christian ministry does not transport any person into another category of human experience."[34]

---

32. Louw, "Compassion Fatigue," 9–10.

33. Bickerton et al., "Well-Being," 9.

34. Fray, *Pain and Joy*, 30.

Chapter 6

Learning to Breathe

Now Nineveh was a very large city;
it took three days to go through it.

—JONAH 3:3B

How does one walk through a large city in three days? Jonah must have had stamina. How are people able to endure many things? I trained for a marathon one year. I ran three to six miles a day and then every other weekend. I did a long run starting with eight miles and building up to twenty-one miles two weeks before the event. Then I went to the race. I started running, but at six miles, I noticed I was struggling. At nine miles, I could hardly catch my breath. I made it to twelve miles, but my breathing was so labored, I had to stop and find help. I was prepared. I trained a year for this event, but I couldn't finish because I couldn't breathe.

Breathing is also important in swimming. Most people breathe incorrectly. Beginners swim and will poke their head straight up out of the water, exhale and inhale, and then place their face back in the water, holding their breath. Breathing like this is an inefficient way to swim and will slow you down, create more drag, and make swimming harder. The result is shallow breathing with a buildup of carbon dioxide in the lungs.[1] The swimmer won't last long. The proper technique is to keep the head, spine, and core aligned. The athlete must rotate the body from the core, lifting the head to inhale, placing it back in the water to exhale, and all in a rhythm of two to three strokes per breath.[2] Swimming requires concentration and fluidity. The breathing rhythm is vital for endurance.

Just like anything that requires fortitude, you must develop the psychological and physical rhythm that can sustain you during your career. Working for God is an endurance sport. God calls people to places, like Jonah preaching to Nineveh; to tasks, like Moses leading the Israelites from Egypt; to people, like Jeremiah prophesying to Israel; and to lifetime service, like the Apostle Paul. When God asks you to serve, that call may be for a few days, a few years, or for life. And there will be barriers along the way. In anticipating those struggles, you can prevent burnout by developing a rhythm of letting go of needless or negative things that weigh you down and taking hold of the good and positive aspects of ministry. Just as the swimmer, or the runner, strips bare of unnecessary items that create resistance and drag, and instead focuses on their actions, thoughts, and responses, so you must do so, all while keeping sight of the finish line. The Apostle Paul reminds us of this, "Therefore, since we are surrounded by such a great cloud of witnesses, let us throw off everything that hinders and the sin that so easily entangles. And let us run with perseverance the race marked out for us, fixing our eyes on Jesus, the pioneer and perfecter of faith."[3] You must breathe out your negative ruminations (obsessive thoughts) and breathe in an expanded view of ministry. You breathe out the binding physical stress and breathe in a nonreactive sense of calm. This rhythm of self-care means increasing consciousness of your self-talk, practicing intentional engagement, and developing a keen awareness of body, emotions, and mindset.

---

1. Gaal, "Proper Breathing," 1.

2. Donovan, "How to Fix," 1.

3. Heb 12:1–2a.

Preventing Emotional Exhaustion

Working in ministry means being with people. Some pastors love to shut their office door, diligent in research and writing, bringing to fruition the next sermon with hopes of notoriety, and great numbers of people swayed by their eloquence. Others love the interaction with important community and political leaders, as doing so elevates their status. However, ask how many ministers enjoy the hospital visits, spending time in the nursing home, or offering counseling to a bickering couple who refuses to listen to any wisdom the leader may have. Or who among clergy enjoy mediating church conflict or managing the politics surrounding church carpeting, pews, or music? Yet, that is a part of the job—working with insecure, often complaining, and sometimes irritating parishioners. Many pastors would love the opportunity to "tell it like it is" to the church. However, their pastoral role constrains them to be kind, caring, and polite.

There are many workers whose jobs require professional behavior in the service of others, from flight attendants to doctors, nurses, and teachers. Professionals must play roles to create positive impressions, and that creates emotional labor.[4] If it's temporary or of short duration, you may have little difficulty in performing, as the role requires surface acting, such as being friendly when you don't feel affable, or smiling when inside you are rushing to the next demanding activity, or being pleasant with a person who has offended you. This acting creates emotional dissonance, a sense that you are faking or wearing a mask.[5] That requires emotional energy. There are differences between genuine smiling and falsely grinning as each use different physiological pathways.[6] Being inauthentic daily for interminable periods is exhausting. You do this throughout the week. Before long, a sense of depletion sets in with feelings of hypocrisy and alienation from your true self.[7]

4. Zapf, "Emotion Work," 238.
5. Zapf, "Emotion Work," 243.
6. Zapf, "Emotion Work," 244.
7. Zapf, "Emotion Work," 245.

Preventing Cynicism

The key becomes consciousness of the disturbance and the story you tell yourself. Staying alert means noticing when your mindset is repeating negative conversations or interactions from the past and bringing those thoughts to the present moment. It means focusing your mind instead of allowing your cognitions to drift into the default of poor regulation and negative mood states.[8] Instead of rehearsing the discomforting emotions, you need to recall the meaning and purpose of small acts of compassion. Those reinvigorate you as those gifted moments remind you that what you do matters, that your words and actions change lives, even if in small ways, and that the present and temporary sacrifice will pay dividends. The renewal of pastoral mission reduces cynicism. Vu and Bodenmann say, "Successfully combating compassion fatigue may require redefinition of our own perceived role and mission as a helping professional . . . it may be necessary to recalibrate our thinking by acknowledging that the use of compassion and empathy can provide us with a high level of professional fulfilment."[9]

Look at my friend Harry as an example. Harry explained that he was exhausted by the church meetings he was required to attend. When I questioned him further, he said, "There are two people who can never agree. I've heard they've never agreed on any church decision as long as they've been members here. It makes the meeting longer, and everyone must endure their jousting until someone calls for a vote. If that happens too soon, these two guys will just continue their debate. It's so tiring. I find myself getting tense and my blood pressure going up just at the thought of the meeting."

I explored Harry's perceptions of the dynamics. Harry interpreted it as conflict and the two men as opponents. I suggested Harry think of this as a checks and balances, where each man represents the collective voice of different groups of people in the church. Somehow these two men are chosen to express opposing

8. Miller and Sprang, "Components-Based Practice," 156.

9. Vu and Bodenmann, "Preventing, Managing and Treating," 228.

views and are representing the whole church. This sparked Harry's interest as he considered that these men were not adversaries, nor did they have conflicting personalities, but were speaking in the service of others. As Harry reframed this, he noticed a change in his physical response. He noted this aloud, and I explained how changing his interpretation of this situation then helped his body alter its perception of the threat.

The conscious acknowledgment of your efforts and creation of a positive narrative become protective factors. As my friend Dan says, "We must remember who we are, whose we are, and where we are going." Once you change the narrative, moving from overburdened to overjoyed, you can engage in listening and offering compassion. This reengagement allows you to offer yourself and invest in ministry, all of which lead to a sense of satisfaction and fulfillment.[10]

When engaged with others, the ministry task shifts to continuous awareness of physical, mental, and emotional experiences. The work with congregants can become intense and painful. In these moments, you can prevent burnout and compassion fatigue with some simple practices by attuning to your physiological responses. You can ask, "How is my body responding in this situation? Am I tense? Is my heart beating faster? Is it harder to breathe?" Those are signs that the sympathetic nervous system of your body is responding to a perceived threat. When your mind thinks you're in danger, even if it's not real, your body shifts into protection mode. The sympathetic nervous system dominates by releasing hormones and enzymes to increase your heart rate, respirations, energy, giving greater strength to your limbs while suppressing your digestive system and numbing your judgment and reasoning.[11] This is helpful if you're crossing a street and a truck comes speeding down the road. You don't need to think—you need to get out of the way quickly. But when you're in a conversation with someone telling about their pain, or in a church meeting that is conflictual, or speaking with a demanding or critical person, your body will respond as if

10. Vu and Bodenmann, "Preventing, Managing and Treating," 228.

11. Gentry and Baranowsky, "Compassion Fatigue," 12.

you're going to be hit by that speeding truck. Learning to manage this physiological arousal will protect you and allow you to think clearly. You can start by breathing deeply, relaxing your muscles or jaw, and slowing the heart rate.[12]

In the act of self-regulation, you are more cognizant of the thoughts and the emotions that are driving the physiological imbalance. As that occurs, acknowledge the discomforting emotions or thoughts, and then focus on nonreactivity. The thoughts can change from "this is overwhelming, and I want to escape," to "I can manage this situation, my efforts will matter, and I will learn something new." Like the waves of the ocean, allow yourself to experience the swell of the distressing emotions, noticing the physical discomfort, not avoiding it, and surfing with the growing uneasiness until it peaks and then flows into peacefulness. Doing so will help you alter the story and change how you encounter the parishioner and the tough situation.[13]

Increasing Personal Efficacy

When burnout occurs and you develop emotional exhaustion and cynicism, you experience a sense that you're not fulfilling your responsibilities at the level expected by yourself or others. You may spend less time on sermon preparation or skip visits to the hospital. You may not be as engaged in the worship experience. Here's how Patricia describes it:

> As I stood up to lead worship, I noticed that I felt utterly detached. I went through the motions and everyone remarked on the wonderful service. But inside I was disappointed with myself. I was disconnected throughout the worship time, from the people, and from God. It wasn't worshipful for me. And that's not typical of me. I was missing the flow and interconnection. Throughout the service, I kept thinking, "You're not doing your job well."

12. Miller and Sprang, "Components-Based Practice," 159.
13. Miller and Sprang, "Components-Based Practice," 158.

Patricia is describing her sense of personal inefficacy, or her low performance. While the members do not recognize it, if it continues, Patricia's disconnection will alter her ministry performance.

The key to prevention lies in engagement and Patricia's self-evaluation. Her negative assessment of herself will distance her from interactions and reinforce any doubts about her ability to perform ministry. When you are experiencing burnout, you have a growing sense of inadequacy, and that will make you feel as if you're not doing your job well. Then you view yourself as a failure which further drains your energy.[14] The result is a self-fulfilling prophecy, because the lack of motivation impacts your functioning. If you can move from self-condemnation to a posture of self-compassion, and engage more fully in your current responsibilities, your sense of satisfaction will increase and serve to protect you.[15]

While you may view this as unfamiliar work, it's critical reflection, skills used in theological education, and spiritual intelligence, which is the awareness, integration, and application of critical reflection in making meaning of a spiritual encounter.[16] In using your ability for deep reflection, a greater sense of purpose and meaning arise, increasing self-awareness, and improving your ability to listen and respond in meaningful ways.[17] There are techniques that increase your spiritual intelligence, improving your persistence, energy, and openness to complexity.[18] Reflective practice means examining your role, experiences as a pastoral leader, your relationships with others, and how you view yourself. Practicing reflection decreases cynicism and restores the core purpose of the work. This allows you to be the isle of peace in a sea of chaos. The skills of consciousness, intentionality, awareness, and non-reactivity operate together in rhythm that provides balance and nourishment, thus preventing burnout and compassion fatigue. The rhythm of breathing, inhaling purpose, exhaling negativity,

14. Maslach and Leiter, "Latent Burnout Profiles," 89.

15. Barnard and Curry, "Relationship of Clergy Burnout," 159.

16. Snelgar et al., "Preventing Compassion Fatigue," 249.

17. Snelgar et al., "Preventing Compassion Fatigue," 249.

18. Snelgar et al., "Preventing Compassion Fatigue," 249.

and all the while giving to the others who are present, sets the pace that protects you in racing to the finish line.

Reflection

The prevention of burnout means maintaining a wholesome perspective and continuous refocusing on redemption. Reflect on the following questions:

1. What aspects of your work bring you the most joy?

2. What practices help you engage more fully in work life and home life?

3. What organizational factors have contributed most to your sense of resiliency for the task of ministry?

4. What guide do you use to make decisions in your ministry? How does that help you maintain perspective?

5. What keeps you in ministry? What helps you most when you are discouraged?

6. What do you need or what would you like to hear from God related to your ministry?

"We are the servants of the Messiah, not the messiahs."[19]

---

19. Willimon, *Clergy and Laity Burnout*, 97.

Chapter 7

Using the Right Gear

When God saw what they did and how they turned
from their evil ways, he relented and did not bring
on them the destruction he had threatened.

—JONAH 3:10

LIFE IS FULL OF surprising twists and turns. It may be impossible
to plan and prepare for all unexpected events, yet it is advisable to
anticipate adverse circumstances. Things may not go as planned,
and if that occurs, you must be prepared. That's what happened
with Jonah. Isn't it a marvelous thing that the city repented because
of Jonah's obedience to God in warning the people? God forgave
Nineveh. It's the best scenario. Yet, it's apparently not what Jonah
expected. He was unprepared for the outcome. Perhaps if Jonah
had considered all the possibilities, he might have reacted differ-
ently. Ministry is akin to open water swimming. Some perils are
known, some creep up suddenly, and some problems cause risks.

In 2010, Fran Crippen, a US national swim team member,
told his coach he wasn't feeling well before an open water race.
He was competing in the FINA Open Water Ten-Kilometer World
Cup near Dubai but did not finish. A search found him almost

two hours later in the water.[1] After an investigation, including an autopsy, the Aquatics Federation made fifty-nine recommendations to cover open water swimming competition. Crippen's death resulted from "cardiac abnormality" and "uncontrolled exercise-induced asthma in unfavorable race environmental conditions." The water was near eighty-six degrees that day.[2] Fran Crippen was not a novice swimmer; he was a world-class athlete. His death was preventable. While some hold the racing event administrators responsible, Fran was also obligated to back out of a race in which he knew beforehand he would be unable to compete.

When swimming in open waters, swimmers are not always properly prepared with the right gear. They'll use their regular swim shorts, no goggles, and will plunge right into the ocean expecting they will be just fine, not realizing that open water swimming differs from swimming in the local pool. Poirier-Leroy recommends the following equipment for open swimming: zinc oxide or sunscreen, open water goggles, a wet suit, swim socks, a bright swim cap, and a swimming buoy.[3] The zinc oxide protects the swimmer's body, and the open water goggles have wider lenses to provide a panoramic view to help with peripheral vision. The wet suit protects the body from irritants in the water while keeping one warm and adds to the body's buoyancy and speed. The swim socks keep the feet and toes warm. Who ever heard of swim socks? The bright swim cap keeps the swimmer visible to passing boaters and the swimming buoy serves as both a safety device and a place to hold on to and rest when tired.[4] All of this gear is protective and preventive. None of it is necessary and so it is easy to underestimate the importance of it. But the gear protects the swimmer from both foreseeable and unknown threats.

Likewise, in ministry, there are prevention measures for compassion fatigue. In chapter 6, I discussed ways to prevent emotional exhaustion, cynicism, and reduced personal efficacy. I

1. Associated Press, "Fran Crippen Dies," 1.

2. Hula, "Fran Crippen Report," 1.

3. Poirer-Leroy, "Beginner's Guide," 1.

4. Poirer-Leroy, "Beginner's Guide," 1.

now turn to the following prevention measures: deepening self-awareness of exposure to trauma, having a support network, and building resilience. To survive open water swimming, you must use the right gear.

Resolving Prior Trauma

All ministers come into the field with various emotional issues. Some are aware of these, while others have yet to discover them. It serves you well to get some counseling from a mental health professional for several reasons, including addressing your personal history and circumstances, and for a deeper understanding of the counseling process for referring church members. You can identify those historical events, or personality factors, that might impact your ministry. Often, professional counselors can discern underlying factors as an outside observer. To illustrate this, I'll use the Johari Window, which was created by psychologists Joseph Luft and Harry Ingham to show different levels of awareness within individuals along two continuums—what is known by others and what is known by yourself.[5] Picture a window with four panes. The upper left pane are those things about you that are known by others and known to you. For example, that known fact may be that you love books, or you are a recent graduate of a program. In the left lower pane, there are things that you keep private from others. So those are things known to you but not by others. Perhaps it's your weight or a medical condition. You may have good reasons for keeping those hidden. In the upper right pane are those things that are known by others but not to yourself. People may know that your tone of voice gets higher when you're irritable, but you may have no awareness of that voice modulation. Finally, in the lower right pane are things, characteristics, hidden agendas, or barriers that are hidden to others and to yourself.[6] One of the goals of psychotherapy is to help you gain more access to those

5. Ramani et al., "Uncovering the Unknown," 1065.
6. Ramani et al., "Uncovering the Unknown," 1067–69.

hidden parts of self to allow you a greater sense of control. They're blind spots and are usually the things that create problems for you in relationships and jobs.

Think about your family of origin, or the family you grew up in, and how all of that has shaped you into who you are now. Every incident, both positive and negative, whether planned or reactionary, even past traumatic church experiences, influence how you interact with others and how you lead. Doolittle says, "Ministers who served a traumatic church in the past were 10.5 times as likely to have high emotional exhaustion, even though they are no longer serving that congregation."[7] Anything that may have been traumatic, or even uncomfortable or awkward, will need some work, and possibly resolution or those will affect your ministry. Here's an example from Colleen:

> As a chaplain, I'm called to pray with patients frequently, especially when they are dying. It's a way of treating others with dignity and respect in their final hours. One time I received a call to pray for a middle-aged man dying who had been an alcoholic for many years. He was dying of alcohol-related disorders and when I saw him a discomforting thought and feeling came upon me. "Why should I pray for you? You did this to yourself! You are responsible for this physical damage!" This dialogue was internal. I would never voice this aloud. But I recoiled that I even had these thoughts or feelings of disdain. Only then did I realize that these thoughts and feelings were left over from my sibling who died as an alcoholic at 48 and who refused any treatment for his alcoholism. At that moment, I realized I had not dealt with my relationship with my brother, his death, and how he lived his life. I noted to take care of that later, and in kindness and with compassion, offered the prayer to the man before me. The incident caught me unaware and ill prepared for the current situation. I committed to resolving that issue to prevent it from creeping up again as I serve other people.[8]

7. Doolittle, "Burnout and Coping," 93.

8. Colleen S., personal communication, July 21, 2002.

Fortunately, Colleen had the awareness of her own emotional and physical reaction to her patient. This helped her to decipher in that exact moment the reason for her distress and redirect that. However, without such awareness and self-regulation, Colleen may have prayed without authenticity, or her spoken words or tone with the patient may have been harsh, or the words of the prayer may have been disrespected.

Increasing Support

Clergy work in isolation even in larger settings. Almost 70 percent of clergy surveyed showed they have no close friend.[9] This isolation occurs sometimes in the development of boundaries with church members and local townspeople, and because of the busyness of the job and physical distance from other clergy. "Many clergy view their family relationships as a primary support system,"[10] yet few realize that this may not serve their family well in the long run. It impacts the minister's spouse and his or her relationship with the congregation and may infect the marital relationship with dread. While it may be helpful to the leader sharing with his or her spouse, it's difficult to be a spouse standing by to watch your loved one treated unfairly or poorly. Here is Sarah's story:

> I remember how hard my spouse struggled to start and maintain a church, a group of people unfamiliar with the denominational practices, and to help them understand the importance of evangelism. He planned and executed successful backyard Bible clubs with over two hundred children attending but received little support from congregants in following up with those children. I heard him criticized for his preaching skills and his management style. As a clergy spouse, I wanted to defend him, especially as several church members surreptitiously began calling on those who had left the church to gather "information" that would speak against him. It took a lot of

9. Meek et al., "Maintaining Personal Resiliency," 342.
10. Jackson-Jordan, "Clergy Burnout," 2.

self-control for me to restrain myself. He resigned after five years of conscientious work, deciding parish ministry was not a good fit. It was probably best because my relationship with the church changed. I no longer trusted the members to support us. My relationship with my spouse also changed. As I watched him struggle, and he noticed my anger rise, he wanted to protect me. Neither of our reactions were beneficial to us individually or as a couple.

So, family support is wonderful but may come with a cost. It can also affect your other family members, such as parents or children. John provides an example of how his church experience impacted his sons.

My sons were raised in the church. I was careful to teach them about God, Christ, and the Bible. They heard and learned all the stories and were involved in Sunday school and youth group. Then I served as an interim pastor for a year. A few years later the same church requested I submit my resume for consideration. I thought it was a great opportunity and had so many ideas for the church. However, during the process, the church was considering other candidates and in visiting the church several times, I was told I was on the "back burner" but still in consideration. Along with that message came complaints about me and my family. In sharing my frustration with my wife, my sons overheard the conversations. Little did I know how this affected them. I was not called to the church. Instead, I was voted down by the congregation. It was wounding. My sons dropped out of church in college with one saying he was uncertain of any belief in God. Eventually the other one began attending again but refuses to darken the door of any church within that denomination. When I asked them about their participation, they both shrugged and remarked that they didn't like the way I was treated. The only things they knew were from overhearing the conversations with my wife.

In seeking support and venting with his family his disappointment and frustration, which were overwhelming at the time,

John infected his sons' perceptions of churches and God. Yet, John needed support from somewhere. Where could he turn?

Many studies show that strong relationships with peers and mentors are a protective factor. Those ministers who meet regularly with such a group have lower emotional exhaustion scores.[11] "We pastors need to know that we are part of something bigger than ourselves and that we, together, are called to a great destiny . . . we need leaders who are themselves excited, themselves energized, themselves passionate about the mission of our church and then personally, enthusiastically communicate that mission to us."[12] Identifying a supportive network of fellow ministers to support you in ministry serves to protect you from burnout or compassion fatigue. Bloom and his team at the Flourishing in Ministry Project at the University of Notre Dame suggest having a mentor.

> Role models are highly credible because they are recognized within a profession for the high quality of their ministry, and so they can provide real, tangible evidence that excellent in ministry is possible. Crucially, role models provide the basis for . . . "possible selves" which are specific, individualized images that people form about the kind of pastor they can hope and strive to become.[13]

The Notre Dame team further states that the more exemplary models you have a connection with, the more you are exposed to a variety of ideas and the more you can gain from those influences. The key is being intentional in your connection to others. It means redirecting your energy away from obsessing on what's going wrong and instead engaging in healthy ways with colleagues.

Building Resiliency

You can build resiliency and reduce your risk for compassion fatigue through the use of self-regulation, intentionality, and

11. Jackson-Jordan, "Clergy Burnout," 2.
12. Meek et al., "Maintaining Personal Resiliency," 343.
13. Bloom et al., "Flourishing," 31.

perceptual maturation (how you perceive yourself and the work-place). Gentry and Baranowsky call these "antibodies."[14] It's not something you regularly think about. While you are aware of self-care habits, like rest, retreat, nutrition, and regular exercise, you are less likely to evaluate your resiliency skills, another form of self-care. Those abilities refer to managing your emotions, validating yourself, developing a sound view of yourself, practicing self-supervision, and focusing your attention on what's most important. These do not automatically occur, nor are they skills that are naturally learned. They require development.

When you have well-developed resiliency, you can flourish despite pressures in a work setting.[15] You can face crisis or stress and move quickly from reactivity to intentionality.[16] The skills of self-regulation are necessary for monitoring your physical reaction to stress. It means learning a new way to talk to yourself, saying, "I know this. This happens to my body and mind when I feel anxiety, or like something or someone is threatening me. But, I'm not in real danger. I can take some deep breaths and relax." The way I explain this to others is that their brain is acting as if there's a hungry tiger in the room. The brain isn't noticing the difference between an actual or perceived threat. I tell people, "Look around the room and then say to yourself, 'There's not a hungry tiger in the room.'" That helps people to regain management of their mind and body.

Practicing self-regulation occurs with intentionality. That requires tuning into yourself. "You cannot be intentional unless you are first aware of what it is that you intend, and that means turning intention into clear, explicit language."[17] This means that one must be mindful. Being mindful and practicing that daily increases empathy and decreases burnout.[18] In listening to stories of suffering, it means asking yourself, "Can I cope with life and suffering? What

14. Gentry and Baranowsky, "Compassion Fatigue," 12–15.

15. Siebert, "Develop Resiliency," 88.

16. Gentry and Baranowsky, "Compassion Fatigue," 13.

17. Gentry and Baranowsky, "Compassion Fatigue," 14.

18. Miller and Sprang, "Components-Based Practice," 155.

is care and how do I care within the awareness of transience and tragedy?"[19] It awakens your conscious intent, making you aware that this is difficult work and there is a follow up in taking care of yourself after listening. I call this self-supervision and it involves the perceptual maturation that Gentry and Baranowsky mention. It means being aware of how you interpret events, situations, and people and recognition of your choices in those times.[20]

Another resiliency practice is spiritual self-care. You face many circumstances that create a paradox. How is it possible to explain why godly people suffer and the unrighteous succeed? How can you respond to the many unanswerable questions that people bring to you? In ministry, you will have circumstances that invade your theological paradigm. What once seemed to have simple answers grows more complex. Listening to those who suffer will pollute your sense of certainty about who you are and what is truth. It can blur your vision until you feel impotent in providing care.[21] Louw suggests that you need to acknowledge the disparity of suffering, continue exercising unconditional love, and use your pastoral caregiving as an opportunity to integrate your spiritual theologies of God, evil, and suffering into your practice.[22] As an evangelist told me in my youth, "Child, you need to stay prayed up." Practicing the spiritual disciplines protects you.

The key in prevention of either burnout or compassion fatigue is awareness of your risk level. Chapters 6 and 7 have mentioned those risks. One final risk remains external to the pastor: church systems. Learning to breathe and wearing the right gear are preparation and preventive methods for open water swimming. However, once in the water, the swimmer faces further obstacles such as the natural swells of the ocean currents. That requires learning navigational skills.

---

19. Louw, "Compassion Fatigue," 3.
20. Gentry and Baranowsky, "Compassion Fatigue," 14–15.
21. Louw, "Compassion Fatigue," 4.
22. Louw, "Compassion Fatigue," 7.

Reflection

There are several ways mentioned in this chapter to prevent compassion fatigue. As you recall those, answer the following questions related to trauma:

1. When you were growing up, what natural disasters did you experience (e.g., tornadoes, fires, windstorms, hurricanes, etc.). How did those impact you?

2. What tragedies did you experience (e.g., loss of a loved one, loss of a job, exposure to a catastrophic event, etc.)? How did these change you?

3. What personal physical injuries, illnesses, or surgeries affected you most?

4. What types of trauma did you experience (e.g., divorce of parents, physical abuse or neglect, sexual abuse, verbal abuse, etc.)? How did that change you?

Now think about the people in your life who were helpful to you as a leader, mentor, or role model. Who were the most influential people? What did you learn from them?

Finally, consider how you respond to stress and answer the following questions:

1. What physical sensations do you experience during stress (e.g., tense jaw, nausea, high blood pressure, etc.)?

2. What do you do with those uncomfortable physical sensations? What helps?

3. How do you respond to conflict? What physical sensations or emotions do you experience?

4. How do you manage your discomfort?

"A preacher should have the mind of a scholar, the heart of a child and the hide of a rhinoceros. His biggest problem is how to toughen his hide without hardening his heart."[23]

23. Thomas, *Practical Wisdom*, 138.

Chapter 8

Navigating the Swells

But to Jonah this seemed very wrong, and he became angry.

—JONAH 4:1

MY, OH MY, THE prophet protests, doesn't he? His anger speaks to his belief about the Ninevites. He may not be wrong. But his emotional reactivity will drain him, as we soon see. He's reacting to a system. Jonah has no vision. He cannot see the end of the plan, God's redemption of all mankind, and so he is drowning in his misery.

Being on the high school swim team was fun. I loved the comradery with fellow swimmers. I enjoyed being competitive. Sometimes I did well; other times I didn't. I was a middle-of-the-pack kind of competitor. But the joy of swimming in competition made up for the lack of winning. I could lose a race, but the entire swim team win a contest. While my individual performance mattered, it was the overall effort of my teammates that made the difference. All the swimming events occurred in pools. I never attempted open water competitions.

Racing in the ocean is different. You need a "high navigational IQ."[1] That means learning to swim the fastest distance in a course. However, that is not always the straightest route. In ocean swimming, you have to understand how the currents, waves, and surface chop impacts your speed and direction. You have to know where the turn buoy rests, where your competitors are at, and the distance to the finish line. All of this requires being fully aware of your surroundings and making a reasonable call about your efforts.[2]

In swimming open waters, you must pay attention to the currents and develop a keen sense of how those are moving. You do so by glancing at the shore to see where anchored boats are pointing and noticing the direction of the wave breaks. Then you adjust your body position. If the waves are pushing left, you may have to swim to the right to stay on course.[3] Sometimes the sun may glare in your eyes, a boat can block your view, or the surface is so choppy, you can't see clearly. That's why bilateral breathing is important; in other words, breathing on both sides, which is difficult to learn, but necessary so you can turn your head away from the intruding sun or crashing wave.[4] A strong navigational IQ grows with an understanding of how the ocean operates, finding new skills to handle the barriers, and practicing those skills. You never swim in the ocean expecting a calm race. That's what makes it exciting. You never know what the open waters will bring.

Operating in a church system is like the open water race. It's possible to chart your way successfully once you have the navigational IQ to survive the breakers of church systems. These skills include an understanding of church systems, how to manage yourself within those systems, and practicing your skills. There may be times when you feel off course, but with practice, you'll find your way to the finish line. I discussed most of the knowledge about church systems in chapter 2, "Barracudas in the Water." However, I'll mention those again so I can identify prevention techniques. The most

1. New Zealand Ocean Swim Series, "Ocean Swimming," 1.
2. New Zealand Ocean Swim Series, "Ocean Swimming," 1.
3. Kostich, "Simple Techniques," 1.
4. New Zealand Ocean Swim Series, "Ocean Swimming," 1.

salient issues that you need to recall are homeostasis, triangulation, family projection and transmission process, and differentiation.

Find Equilibrium

The church (or any other) system is intent on surviving, and you must maintain that as a guiding philosophy to help you in charting a course of direction to prevent burnout or compassion fatigue. You need a clearly defined role that fits you, offers you high satisfaction in the job, and provides you with adequate rewards. Some systems lack what it takes to provide you with those. Changing an organization is difficult. Resistance occurs when you attempt to make changes too quickly, or when you try to adjust too much, or too often, or when you try to modify something important to the group. Systems resist changes, either through their policies, their board, their formal statements or rules of organizations, or through the pushback or silence or lack of cooperation you receive. In time, this will cause burnout as you realize that you have little control over the outcomes and begin to over-function in your responsibilities. Most of this occurs before the system assimilates you, and before you've completed negotiations for your leadership. "Each local church is a unique system, and leadership is something that emerges and happens in the unique systemic situation of a particular church. Leadership cannot emerge until a person has taken his or her place in the system both to influence and be influenced by the system."[5]

There are three dynamic principles in operation that pertain to homeostasis: wholeness, synergy, and isomorphism (similarities in vision and purpose or complementary views of those).[6] Wholeness refers to the concept that the sum of the parts is greater than the individual parts, or the organization or church as a whole is more powerful than any individual member. You must become part of the whole so you can be a productive influencer. As you do

5. Stevens and Collins, *Equipping Pastor*, 4.
6. Stevens and Collins, *Equipping Pastor*, 4–6.

so, then you will experience the synergy, or powerful interaction, that occurs when people work together harmoniously. It means allowing the system to influence you while you try to change it. This will occur only as there are either similarities or complementary views of the organization's mission. If your vision and the church's vision are similar, alteration will occur more readily as the members learn to trust that you have their best interests in mind. You can still alter the system if your view is different, but only if it complements or adds to their ideology. If it's too dissimilar, then change will not occur.[7] That's what happened to Darren. "When I accepted a call to be senior pastor at a church, I was told by several people it was a *pastor-killing* church. I made so many rookie mistakes, moved too fast, and didn't see the underground leadership network. In the fifth year of my tenure, I learned of secret meetings, and then the personnel committee asked me to leave."[8]

To prevent burnout, you must have reasonable expectations that you will not join the system for a while. Nothing will happen successfully until you have passed through several stages of acceptance from the congregation, which typically takes about three years.[9] The best thing you can do is aid the church in its desire to accomplish its purpose. You do this in your supportive words and actions. Remind yourself that resistance to change is the system's response to anxiety. It's imperative you never underestimate the power of homeostasis. You will be tested, and triangulation will occur.

Deal with Triangulation

It is impossible to avoid triangulation. The nature of your leadership role places you squarely in the path of managing the church's or members' anxiety. Think of all the possible triangles that can occur:

- Pastor-Staff-Congregation
- Pastor-Deacons-Vision for church

7. Stevens and Collins, *Equipping Pastor*, 4–6.
8. Darren N., personal communication, March 7, 2012.
9. Stevens and Collins, *Equipping Pastor*, 10.

- Pastor-Staff Member 1-Staff Member 2
- Pastor-Vision-Congregation resistance
- Pastor-Staff-Member
- Pastor-Member-Member

This is not an exhaustive list. Triangulation, or being pulled in the middle, is neither good nor bad. It's a matter of how people function when they experience anxiety. Triangulation can calm anxiety, but if it inhibits change, then it's unhealthy. If the result is growth or resolution, then triangles can be healthy in a system.

To prevent burnout, you must develop an awareness of when triangulation is occurring, respond without emotional reaction, and then move the person to a healthier conversation. In his book *Generation to Generation*, Edwin Friedman provides the following example: "Woman to minister after she had dropped him off at home, following a meeting: 'Mr. Williams, I just want you to know that there are some members of this congregation who are out to get you, but I'm on your side.'"[10] It's so enticing, isn't it? You want to know which members, or what did they say? Mr. Williams's congregant is pulling him into the middle of a triangle. The only purpose it serves is to ease her anxiety about what others are saying while increasing the minister's worry. The key here is to de-triangulate. That can occur in several ways. Think about the minister's options in responding. He could say, "Oh? Well, why don't you plan a meeting with them and see what the hubbub is about." Or, he could say, "Hmm. Suppose you let them know of your discomfort and allegiance." Either way, the minister is refusing to accept her unease, or rescue her of her qualms, and giving her the responsibility for taking action. This is a skill you can learn as you understand more clearly the family projection process.

10. Friedman, *Generation to Generation*, 213.

Manage Family Process

Murray Bowen's theory of family systems and, subsequently, Edwin Friedman's theory of church systems propose that the key factor driving the organization is anxiety. Fears dominate us at times, and when our uncertainties pool with the reservations of others, it becomes what seems an overwhelming force. Then the combined anxiety is so overpowering that if the church cannot bear the load, it will seek to cast it upon you. "As anxiety in a system increases, responses become more exaggerated. Therefore, in a time of declining church membership and finances, anxiety increases. As anxiety increases, more pressure is put on the clergy to perform and turn things around."[11] This apprehension is dramatized as the individual members and you act out of your assigned roles that originated in your families of origin. If a church member was the hero, they will attempt to rescue the system or someone within the system. If they were the lost child, they'll either try to garner attention or run away to hide. If they were the rebellious child, they will resist everything. In addition, they will need to throw the unrest upon someone. Most likely, they will blame you or give you full responsibility for reducing the joint anxiety.

The two danger areas for you in the family projection process is over-functioning for the congregation and being emotionally reactive. Being a church or organization leader is an opportune place to receive affirmation and appreciation when things go well. Unfortunately, when you rely upon this positive feedback and attempt to continue receiving this idealization, then you will face rising feelings of insecurity or inadequacy. The congregation will not always applaud, and when that confirmation ceases, you are left to assume that you are not pleasing the people. You will then engage in behavior that seeks to gratify the ideal expectations of the church, which becomes harder as time goes by, and ultimately leads to burnout.[12] Ensuring a sustaining career means that you must refrain from seeking the attention of the congregation.

11. Grosch and Olsen, "Clergy Burnout," 624.
12. Grosch and Olsen, "Clergy Burnout," 621.

Instead, you need to move from holding primary responsibility for the success of the church mission to aiding the members to distribute that responsibility among themselves. Instead of encouraging neediness, you lead the congregants to interdependence. As a healthy preacher, you recognize the importance of organizing people around a mission instead of simply inspiring the church.[13]

The other hazard, emotional reactivity, moves you into a stance of defense. Jonah makes this mistake as his agenda for Nineveh is short-circuited by God's redemptive act, and Jonah responds in anger. This is akin to the open water swimmer trying to reach the destination while swimming against the tide. It takes more effort and will only end up causing greater fatigue. Friedman says,

> The capacity of members of the clergy to contain their own anxiety regarding congregational matters, both those not related to them, as well as those where they become the identified focus, may be the most significant capability in their arsenal. Not only can such capacity enable religious leaders to be more clear-headed about solutions and more adroit in triangles but . . . a nonanxious presence will modify anxiety throughout the entire congregation.[14]

It is in being a non-anxious presence, that you can exert more influence on the entire system.

There are two primary ways to do this. First, focus on process instead of content. You can also use playfulness. During times of conflict, most often people concentrate on the exact words being said and whether those are true, helpful or not helpful, or right or wrong. Those dichotomies become splitting and soon people are arguing about the argument. You can alter the conversation by changing the focus to process, or rather to the feelings of fear that the people are facing. In that way, you teach them how to listen for the sake of understanding, instead of listening to win. At other times, you can add some playfulness with carefully placed humor.

---

13. Steinke, *Healthy Congregations*, 44–45.

14. Friedman, *Generation to Generation*, 208.

This decreases the tone of seriousness and lightens the mood.[15] However, this only happens with an adequate level of differentiation.

Gain Differentiation

In any religious organization, your role as spiritual leader is aiding in the development and activation of the mission. You must lay aside any personal agenda and join with the people. That means becoming part of the group but not necessarily intertwined in the crowd. You accomplish this through de-triangulation and nonreactivity and then maintain that while assisting the church in its goals. It means being clear about your role and function. Differentiation means maintaining a non-anxious presence instead of a reactive one, using more cognitive or thinking skills instead of emotional ones.[16] The genuine test of your differentiation is how you react amid challenge. In doing so, you choose what is best for the entire system rather than what the individual desires. It means remaining committed to the church's overall vision rather than yielding to one member's idea. It requires you be an individual while being part of a group, thereby demonstrating interdependence.

Differentiation releases you from bearing more of the emotional burden for the church than is necessary. It defines the leadership role more clearly, moving from role ambiguity which increases the risk for burnout, shifting the work overload to a shared load with congregants, and developing realistic expectations for all leaders. It teaches and affirms that the church can address or deal with its own issues, and that a healthy congregation recognizes that disturbance and conflict is natural, and not a predictor of failure.[17]

Navigating the church system leads to a successful finish when you recognize the importance of homeostasis, deal with triangulation, manage the family projection process, and gain differentiation.

15. Friedman, *Generation to Generation*, 209–10.

16. Friedman, *Generation to Generation*, 228–29.

17. Steinke, *Healthy Congregations*, 10.

Like the bilateral breathing that accompanies the frequent sightings, these practices help you to stay on course through the squalls, the tides, and the blinding sun of ministry work.

Reflection

Learning to manage family systems in a church takes time and thoughtfulness. Think about the following:

1. How would you describe the stages of acceptance for you to be inducted into the ministry system?

2. What are your patterns of communication? What is the church's pattern? Are the two blending?

3. What types of triangulation do you often find yourself in? How do you respond?

4. What might be some safe methods to help identify the "barracudas" in your system?

5. How can you achieve differentiation? What does that mean to you?

6. What are the risks and gains from differentiation?

"The interrelatedness of life means that we will always deal with emotional processes. As levels of anxiety increase, we become more instinctual. It's a matter of survival. Power struggles, jealousies, betrayals, splits, and other forms of broken boundaries ensue. And what was operative in the biblical world is at work today. The stories are mirrors, reflections of our own world."[18]

---

18. Steinke, *How Your Church Family Works*, 119.

Part III

The Rescue

Jonah had gone out and sat down at a place east of the city.
There he made himself a shelter, sat in its shade and
waited to see what would happen to the city.

—JONAH 4:5

DROWNING OCCURS WHEN A swimmer continues despite fatigue
and cramping muscles. The diver who goes too deep with insufficient air or rises too quickly will face trouble. Swimming beyond
one's capacity is a setup for failure. We need to watch over one
another to provide adequate supervision. This was never more
clear than when my grandson was learning to swim. At a family
event, we skipped down to the private pool. My grandson was so
excited to swim with us. But he stayed at the water's edge. He was
afraid to come into the pool. I swam to him and reassured him I
would keep him safe. I coaxed him until he held out his arms, and
with his floatie around his waist, we crept into the pool. I gently
bounced him in the water while guiding him around. His grip on
me was tight, but soon I saw him smiling. Over the next few days,
we repeated this scene, and I kept him safe. I did not allow him to
go to the water alone. While his wariness protected him, I wanted

to ensure that his growing confidence did not deceive him into taking risky chances. He was vulnerable, and if I left him at the pool alone, his growing courage might win over his cautiousness where he might dive in over his head.

Jonah's ministry leads him to exhaustion. He's drowning in his expectations and needs rescue and resuscitation. His focus is on the city as he awaits its destruction. His anger is symptomatic of his worldview. Does he recognize he needs to look to God? Does he know he's at risk? How do you know if you're experiencing burnout or compassion fatigue? What symptoms are evident in ministry leaders? And if you are experiencing burnout or compassion fatigue, what steps should you take? The rescue at sea, or treatment for burnout and compassion fatigue, require a coordination of efforts: resuscitation (reappraisal, restoration, refreshment, and renewal), saving yourself (techniques, intentionality, building a support network), and sharing the buoys (help for spouses). Like Jonah, you need shelter from the glaring sun, and you need to move your focus from ministry to God.

Jonah is not alone in the biblical figures who struggle with burnout or compassion fatigue. Elijah's story illustrates burnout and shows the path of resuscitation through rest, retreat, self-examination, worship, and renewed calling. Without a doubt, the weary minister needs rest from the work. Wayne Muller says, "I had always assumed that people I loved gave energy to me, and people I disliked took it away from me. Now I see that every act, no matter how pleasant or nourishing, requires effort, consumes oxygen. Every gesture, every thought or touch, uses some life."[1] You need Sabbath rest. To honor the Sabbath means more than worshipping in church. It requires that you stop and acknowledge the need to be still and surrender. In resting, you cease to be indispensable and instead realize you are not responsible for everything but there are larger forces at work in the universe. It is a reminder of your place in God's economy and that produces contentment.[2]

1. Muller, *Sabbath*, 8.
2. Muller, *Sabbath*, 65.

In resting, you retreat. Elijah travels to Mount Horeb, a place one might consider a sacred space, a place where one senses a connection greater than oneself.[3] It means a return to a time or place or memory of a spiritual encounter with God. It is a time when God spoke clearly to you while you gained a definitive sense of God's presence. In this solitude, you rekindle the flame that is burning low.[4] Examine your calling. In 1 Kings 19, God asks Elijah, "What are you doing here?"[5] What an odd question. God asked Elijah to meet at this place but is now leading him to examine his heart, motivation, and purpose. Elijah's response reflects his inner turmoil. He expresses his frustrations, fears, exhaustion, and sense of abandonment. The question probes further: *Why are you here?* It is the existential question of meaning that leads Elijah directly to the heart of God. When you neglect this watchful soul care, and lose touch with yourself, then you are lost at sea. But if you practice self-awareness and critical reflection, examine your ministry and faith, and recall your central purpose, you will find energy and strength and an integrated faith. This practice provides you with clarity in decisions and highlights areas of growth. It points out your motivations and uncovers ways for you to distinguish the role of minister from person. It serves to reassure you and provide you direction for the future.

During retreat, you can move into worship to experience God's presence. While Elijah stands at the mouth of the cave waiting for God's movement, he discovers something new. God does not appear in the wind, earthquake, or fire, but in the "eerie silence."[6] Elijah finds God in the moment's stillness. It reminds the prophet of God's magnificence and expands Elijah's vision that God is present, even when unseen or unheard. It is a fresh encounter that leads to wholeness. Worship changes your view of life and prepares you to respond to God's dream for you, and the expansion of vision empowers you to renew your calling.

3. Adelstein, "Sacred Space," 1.
4. Nouwen, *Way of the Heart*, 55.
5. 1 Kgs 19:9–10.
6. Wiener, *Prophet Elijah*, 14.

Before Elijah leaves Mount Horeb, God provides a helper, Elisha, and offers hope and a renewed sense of purpose for Elijah's ministry. Having a supportive network and understanding the meaning of your ministry carries you through the most difficult circumstances. Viktor Frankl said, "One should not search for an abstract meaning of life. Everyone has his own specific vocation or mission in life to carry out a concrete assignment that demands fulfillment. Therein he cannot be replaced, nor can his life be repeated. Thus, everyone's task is as unique as is his opportunity to implement it."[7]

Once you can grasp a greater sense of purpose, then a renewed hope and compassion for people returns. The anticipation in a transformed calling is less about others' opinions, success, or your feelings, and instead is based on an enduring hope that God walks with you. In regaining your calling, your distorted perception clears. Your mind is reopened to accepting your followers and you experience a restoration to leadership. Along with this is a change in your thinking and how you accomplish things. Ellen Charry says that God's goal is to renew your mind and to refocus, reminding you of who you really are.[8] In so doing, you learn the requisite resiliency skills while practicing authenticity and thriving in ministry.[9]

---

7. Frankl, *Man's Search for Meaning*, 110–11.

8. Charry, *By the Renewing of Your Minds*, 93.

9. Bloom, *Flourishing in Ministry*, 2.

Chapter 9

Resuscitation

Then the Lord God provided a leafy plant and made it grow up
over Jonah to give shade for his head to ease his discomfort,
and Jonah was happy about the plant.

—JONAH 4:6

HOW DOES A PERSON know if they are drowning? Does it take much
to drown? Think you're safe around water? Actually, it doesn't take
a lot of water for drowning. It depends on your age, weight, and
breathing ability. Some studies show that a person weighing one
hundred forty pounds can drown in as little as a quarter cup of water, if inhaled.[1] Here's how to know you're in trouble. If you swallow water, you will become anxious and your body will move to
a fight-or-flight state as you struggle with breathing. Your airway
tightens to prevent more water from coming in, so you uninten-
tionally hold your breath. After two minutes, you will likely lose
consciousness. This is when you need resuscitation.[2] Recognition
of the initial drowning signs is key.

1. Watson, "Drowning Facts," 1.
2. Watson, "Drowning Facts," 1.

Many spiritual leaders are unaware when they're in trouble. They assume it's natural to feel emotional exhaustion and ineffective at times.[3] Often pastors are so busy they ignore the early signs of burnout or compassion fatigue. They think that a day off to detach or a good night's rest will help. While those are good ideas, they will not alleviate the chronic exhaustion, creeping depersonalization, or decreasing productivity. This is the time to assess for burnout or compassion fatigue.

Assessment

Burnout is so gradual that it sneaks up on you. Pastors describe it as spiritual exhaustion, discouragement, or frustration. They speak of an inability to care or as if they have emotional bankruptcy. Clergy express feelings of self-doubt or inadequacy. They talk of wanting to quit. Others notice the minister is withdrawn and less fruitful than previously. How do you know if you have burnout? Scott Nichols, pastor of Crossroads Church in Carol Stream, Illinois, says his signs include avoiding people even though he's an extrovert, cancelling meetings, procrastinating, pushing deadlines, impatience, and increasing temptations.[4] The following symptoms are key:

- Emotional exhaustion
- Cynicism
- Lack of caring
- Loss of humor
- Dissatisfaction with ministry, disillusionment
- Loss of enthusiasm
- Increasing frustration, irritability, or anger
- Feeling stagnation or apathy

3. Bloom, *Flourishing in Ministry*, 19.
4. Nichols, "Pastors & Burnout," 1.

- Feeling inadequate

- Lower productivity

- Poor morale

- Unexplained sadness

- Impatience

If you have several of those, you probably need further assessment. One tool created for clergy is the Clergy Burn-Out Inventory developed by Roy Oswald. It's a short survey with sixteen questions designed to assess your level of burnout. It's available and free for public use.[5]

Compassion fatigue may appear suddenly or gradually, depending on whether you are also experiencing burnout. It is possible to experience both at the same time. Additional symptoms that indicate compassion fatigue include:

- Faster heart rate or rising blood pressure when thinking of or in contact with certain individuals

- Desire to avoid any thoughts, memories, or contact with suffering individuals

- Using a silencing response with others so you don't have to offer care or counseling

- Intrusive thoughts of a time when helping someone

- Nightmares or frequent dreams of the person you are counseling or of the encounter

- Diminished concentration

Ministry leaders who care and listen to those who are suffering are exposed to the person's trauma. It's like a contagious virus. Upon hearing the story, it's difficult to get the pictures out of your mind. To further determine if you have compassion fatigue, you can use the Professional Quality of Life Scale, otherwise known as the ProQOL, which is the most widely used tool to determine

5. Oswald, "How Dry," 1.

compassion fatigue, compassion satisfaction, and burnout.[6] (See bibliography for further information.)[7]

Whether you have burnout or compassion fatigue, the treatment begins with restoration of your relationship with God and renewal of your calling. It's not enough to reduce the ministry demands. The healing comes in reengaging in the importance, significance, and purpose of your work.[8] Doing your faith work is necessary for healing.

Restoration

During Jonah's exhaustion, God provides him with a place to rest that provides protection. If you are burned out or have compassion fatigue, you also need rest. While a sabbatical is wonderful, it's not a possibility for all ministers. However, let's think about what you actually need. If you're emotionally exhausted, the rest you need is a balance of activities that require emotional strength and those that give you energy. It involves a mix of demands and resourceful acts. It's a rhythm of work and rest. Just as the swimmer cannot simply stop swimming to reach the shore, so you must continue in your efforts. The swimmer uses the rhythm of his or her actions to provide short moments of rest mixed with bursts of energy. Look for those things that feed your soul. Is it a particular sport or game? Do you gain fulfillment from reading, writing, or an artistic activity? Perhaps it's something that brings you happiness, or it may be something challenging, like learning a new language or taking a course in management. Resting for the sake of burnout is less about sleeping or getting away than it is about learning a new flow in life. "Flow is being completely involved in an activity for its own sake. The ego falls away. Time lies. Every action, movement, and thought follows inevitably from the previous one, like playing jazz. Your

---

6. Stamm, *Concise ProQOL Manual*, 8.

7. Stamm, "Professional Quality of Life Scale," 1.

8. Bickerton, "Well-Being," 5.

whole being is involved, and you're using your skills to the utmost."[9]
Creating flow uplifts your spirit and refreshes your soul.

Taking regular breaks throughout the day to do those things
that replenish you is as important as multiple days away. Those
times allow you to recharge.[10] When you practice this rhythm of
rest, you experience a higher level of authenticity, being true to
yourself and expressing yourself in ways consistent with your inner being. Bloom calls this a "restorative niche." It involves something you do well or can master and you do it simply for the joy
of the experience itself.[11] The idea is not in doing less, but doing
more of what you love, intermingled with your job demands. It is
then you realize your ministry is not something to do but rather
an act of who you are.

Refreshment

The next step in resuscitation is refreshing your soul. Oftentimes,
ministry leaders neglect their personal spiritual life in leading
religious organizations. My friend John, who oversees a group of
clergy, says that pastors have a tendency to read the Bible for the
sake of sermon preparation, and not for their personal growth.
Their prayers center on the needs of the people, instead of being
an intimate conversation with God for their own sake. Yet when
clergy are asked what benefits them most and protects them from
burnout or compassion fatigue, they reply it is their practice of
spiritual disciplines.[12]

The disciplines are spiritual activities that nourish your connection with God. It's vital you continually examine your relationship with God. Are you listening for God's personal word to you?
Are you growing in intimacy with God? How are you doing this? Is
your bond with God healthy? Explore your view of God and how

9. Csikszentmihalyi, *Flow*, 28.

10. Bickerton, "Well-Being," 5.

11. Bloom, "Flourishing," 18.

12. Bloom, "Flourishing," 21.

you believe God views you. Recently, the pastor of my church asked the members, "What do you think is God's first thought of you?" My response immediately was, "I'm doing alright. God is pleased with me." However, other members stated words like "disappointed," "frustrated," and "neglectful." I thought that was so sad.

In the process of burning out or experiencing the trauma of working with people, you lose the understanding of how the world operates and how God works. When you don't see justice in the way you expect, just as Jonah, you lose perspective. Gentry and Block remind us, "This carves deep spiritual and moral wounds by shattering the essential, largely unstated assumptions about ourselves and the world around us that imbue our lives with meaning and purpose."[13] No longer is the ministry a place where right equals might, and wrong is condemned. It leaves you confused about how to provide care in a topsy-turvy world, even when you depend upon God. It causes a loss of hope and disappointment with the Holy One. Does God hear your cries for help? Does God really care for the righteous? In what way is God connecting with the human dilemma, or to you?

Having a sense of connection to God and feeling God's loving acceptance is part of recovery. It lightens your load when you know that God is for you, working with you, and has not abandoned you. Jesus's words remind you to abide in him because he abides in you.[14] When you have that sense of God in you, then you have assurance that God is walking alongside to help carry your load. Jesus tells you that in your weariness, he will provide rest, that his yoke is easy, and the burden is light.[15] But it takes two to carry the yoke—you and God. You don't have to push and pull to make things happen. Richard Rohr says, "Faith does not need to push the river precisely because it is able to trust that there is a river. The river is flowing; we are already in it."[16] Rohr reminds you that you are part of something far bigger than yourself. You are

13. Gentry and Block, *Forward Facing Trauma Therapy*, loc. 738.

14. John 15:1-5.

15. Matt 11:28-30.

16. Rohr, "Trust," 1.

part of God's entire redemption plan and that God is the source, not you. When you feel you cannot do one more thing, it's time to cease striving and trust God is proactive. God sees and knows what is needed in every circumstance. You can only do this when you reconnect with God.

Renewal

Being in ministry should be a collaborative venture. Sometimes leaders take positions of deferring to God, passively moving all responsibility to God, while others assume too much self-direction. Understanding that you work with and for God restores a sacred partnership.[17] God has not abandoned you. In what ways do you engage your faith in your ministry? Do you "suck it up" and try to do it alone? Or do you cultivate your relationship with God, clarifying your role as different than God's job? What does God expect of you? What has God called you to do? That's where Jonah is confused. God tells Jonah to preach a message of repentance. That's the only job God requires. God's responsibility is dealing with the people's responses. Jonah becomes angry at Nineveh and God. He's confusing his role.

Have you done that before? I remember someone asking how my book sales were going. I explained, "God didn't call me to sell books. That's God's job. God called me to write books." Whenever I fall into the trap of role confusion, that's when I work too hard and am unhappy that my results are less than I expect. Then I remind myself, "That's not your job. Stick to what you're called to do." How often in your life have you confused your calling with the results? Gary Bickerton says, "Cultivating a sense of what it is specifically that one has been sovereignly placed by God in the position to do, together with collaborating with God in the ups and downs of seeking to do it, directly aid well-being in ministry regardless of one's personality type."[18]

17. Bickerton, "Well-Being in Ministry," 9.
18. Bickerton, "Well-Being in Ministry," 10.

When you experience either burnout or compassion fatigue, it's time to reexamine your calling. Somehow, you've lost authenticity. Yet, being true to yourself and God's calling means you are serving in a way consistent with your inner thoughts and feelings. That's when your job fulfillment and compassion satisfaction rise.[19] When you are satisfied and happy in your work, you bring your best self to the job. Your performance improves and you become a motivational presence. It is when you are fully engaged. "Engagement captures experiences that occur when people are able to draw upon and utilize their greatest physical, cognitive, spiritual and emotional resources and direct their best energies into their work. When people can give their fullest and best to an activity, given the resources that activity requires, they are fully engaged."[20] But authenticity only occurs when you have a deep sense of your values and beliefs, of your strengths and weaknesses, and clarity about your calling.

God asks Elijah, "Why are you here?" It's the question you must answer. Why are you in your place of ministry? Did God call you there or did you accept the position for any other reason? What motivated you to accept your current position? Go back to your initial calling to ministry. What was God's word to you? Consider other questions: Does this job fit who you are? Would another place be better? Or is there something within you that needs to change in this place? When you gain clarity about your purpose in ministry, it becomes the internal compass that helps you stay on course.[21]

This means that you must meet God face-to-face, or on your knees, to seek a fresh anointing. When Jesus faced exhaustion, he would slip into the wilderness and pray.[22] You may think that odd. If Jesus only had a limited time in ministry, how could he possibly spend any of that time alone? Was it to set an example or was there a deeper reason? Here's what Spaite says: "The reason Jesus often

19. Bloom, *Flourishing*, 44.
20. Bloom, *Flourishing*, 45.
21. NCLS Research, "Leadership," 1.
22. Luke 5:16.

took time away to rest and pray was because he could not fulfill his calling unless he did."[23] Spaite says it provides you with an example. I think it shows you must be alone in stillness with the Holy One so you can be free from external voices and demands crying for your attention. It is a time where you face yourself, your struggles, and your needs in light of God's grace. It's the time when God not only asks, "Why are you here?" but "What are you called to do" and "Who is calling you?" Why do you want to be a minister? In what way does it make you feel better about yourself?

There are times when people come into church leadership seeking affirmation, importance, or out of a need to be wanted or needed. Or they choose the career because someone said they should be a preacher, or they felt pressured by someone. Sometimes the Holy Spirit uses those people, while at other times the motivation to minister is based on unconscious feelings or needs. Why are you here? It's scary to face these questions, isn't it? Louis McBurney says, "There looms the threat to our faith, since we believed firmly that God was leading and in control. We must also face the uncertainty that change of direction might entail. However, once this confession is made to self, it becomes less threatening to share it with someone else."[24] During the silence, it is time to listen to God. Ask God, "Did you invite me or was I simply inducted? What do you have in mind? Tell me how you want to use me." Then wait until you hear the eerie silence. In the moment of absolute stillness, God will speak.

Reflection

As you focus on your need for rest and a renewed calling to ministry, answer the following questions:

1. In what ways do you honor the Sabbath? How do you seek to provide moments of rest?

23. Spaite and Goodwin, *Time Bomb*, 125.
24. McBurney, *Every Pastor*, 32.

2. How did the word of the Lord related to your ministry calling come to your attention?

3. What images connect to your view of your calling to be a human vessel for a divine message?

4. What thoughts anchor reassurance of God's call on your life to ministry?

5. In what ways do you resist God's call on your life?

6. Think about a time when you experienced God's promise of empowerment. What thoughts and feelings did you have at the time?

"We ought daily to renew our vows, and to kindle our hearts to zeal, as if each day were the first day of our conversion."[25]

25. Kempis, *Imitation of Christ*, 41.

Chapter 10

Saving Yourself

But the Lord said, "You have been concerned about this plant,
though you did not tend it or make it grow. It sprang up
overnight and died overnight."

—JONAH 4:10

SUBMERSION IN WATER ISN'T always fatal. Jaime Rios tells his story
of losing control of his truck and plunging into the water. Here's
his description,

> They say that in a near-death experience, your life flashes
> before your eyes. Every thought I've ever had, every feel-
> ing I've ever felt, rushes in. . . . It takes all my remaining
> willpower to put those thoughts and feelings aside and
> concentrate on the task at hand. . . . It's then I realize
> the water level has stopped rising and is holding at two
> inches from the ceiling of the truck. "I'm going to try
> harder," I respond.[1]

Jaime saved himself from drowning, but he had to think
clearly, plan an escape route, find the right technique, and persevere

---

1. Rios, "I Was Seconds Away," 1.

until he escaped. That is the lesson for anyone who is nearly drowning: developing a plan, using good equipment, and determination.

Janet came seeking help. As associate minister in a midsize congregation, her responsibility was providing pastoral care and counseling to church members and their families. Visiting the sick and lonely in hospitals and nursing homes took a large part of Janet's time. She also called on those who could not leave their home because of their frailty, or other reasons. In her pastoral caregiving, she offered solace to those who were grieving, encouragement to members who were despairing, and consolation to those who were hurting. A large part of her time involved listening to stories. Many of those were heartbreaking.

> One day I was listening to a church member share her story of domestic violence. She described how her spouse grabbed her and pulled her by the hair down a flight of stairs. And then she told me how he punched her in the face, leaving a large, swollen mark around the eye. The woman had missed church recently because she didn't want to explain why she was bruised. I remember as she was describing, I felt sick at my stomach, and then I went numb. I couldn't feel anything, or even really hear the woman. It was as if my ears had plugs in them. I could hear sounds, but not the woman's words. I felt such a deep anger—at her (why didn't she leave), at her spouse (what a jerk), at God (how could God let this happen), and at me for not having solutions. I was speechless. I prayed with the woman, but I don't even remember the words I used because I was so disconnected at that point. I need help. Give me a plan to work through this so I can be useful in ministry again.

Wisely, Janet realized she could not do this on her own and so I outlined a plan for her. If you are experiencing something similar, or have lost the joy of your ministry, I recommend a plan that includes becoming intentional, building resiliency, and finding connection and support.

Become Intentional

Serving in churches or religious organizations means spending a lot of time in planning and serving. Situations arise that need your attention, and before you've had a minute to think, you're off to the next event, the next visit, or another meeting. It's as if your life is planned for you. The problem is that it leaves you sensing a lack of control which impacts your efforts at caring for your body, mind, and spirit. In the whirl of activities, the time you meant to spend quietly with God, or in renewing your spirit fall aside. In recovery, it's important you develop intentionality. That requires purposefully planning and guarding the things that support your well-being. It means practicing the skills you need and planning your response in advance.

Intentionality requires spiritual intelligence and intrinsic motivation. Spiritual intelligence is the ability to be aware of one's inner world (thoughts, feelings, physical sensations) while attuning to the outer world (things that are happening, what people are saying and doing). It means adapting one's responses to the ongoing situation with thoughtful reflection, recognizing the overarching meaning and purpose and how it connects to others. It's transcending your current state of being. Along with this, intrinsic motivation, or the desire to do something that arises from within you, instead of being an obligation, brings a higher level of interest, excitement, passion, and confidence.[2]

Intentionality best occurs when you develop a mission statement based upon your retreat with God. One of the best activities I did during my recovery came from this idea. During my retreat, I asked God for clear direction for the next two years. Once I was certain about this, I sat and wrote "My Mission Statement." It was a short page of several paragraphs but as I wrote it, I thought of what it entailed and ruled out what didn't fit. Shortly after doing this activity, a close friend called to ask me to participate in an event. I became excited as we talked about it, knowing it was an area of interest and I had the talent to do it. During the conversation an

2. Snelgar et al., "Preventing Compassion Fatigue," 247.

inner voice said, "Does this fit your mission for the year?" I hesitated, and then told my friend about my mission statement. Then I declined the invitation. It was difficult to do so but I realized the request was stroking my ego but not fitting the clarity of vision I gained with God. In doing this, I felt a lightness I had never experienced. I wasn't bound to duty or obligation, nor was I entangled in my own interests and needs. I felt free and focused.

Being intentional is also about clarifying your actions on a daily and weekly basis by setting goals for your recovery. Intentionality is essential in setting boundaries and creating balance in your life. You practice it when you separate who you are from the role of minister, creating a separateness and claiming your independence. You observe the importance of being deliberate when you acknowledge and attune to your inner thoughts and feelings. It leads you to ask questions like, "What will I do with this pain?" It is self supervision as you notice and observe both your inner and outer experiences, noting when you need to deal with something further. Intentionality leads you, just like it did Jane, to recognize when you are not fully present, and to process a situation to fully metabolize or work through your discomfort physically, cognitively, and spiritually. As you practice intentionality, your resilience will develop.

Build Resilience

Compassion fatigue and burnout arise from a lack of resiliency, meaning a lack of mindfulness, self-regulation, and a failure to manage spiritual and personal meaning-making. God provided plenty of shade and comfort for Jonah. However, in Jonah's obsession with what was happening to Nineveh, he neglected to care for the plant. What might have happened if Jonah had focused on the present moment and his immediate surroundings? He needed to attend to the things that were refreshing his spirit. When you intentionally practice these skills, your resiliency grows, and your spiritual life deepens. When you don't do these things, the result weakens your limited resources, resulting in spiritual dryness. You may be spiritual but lack spiritual vitality.[3] Emotional exhaustion inhibits your ability to transcend limits, to reason, be creative, and distorts your perception of yourself and others.[4] The goal in recovery is becoming mindful, practicing self-regulation, and changing your view of yourself and the world around you.

Chronic stress and exposure to dismal stories not only have an emotional impact, but a physical affect. Your body can withstand great pressure or stress during a crisis. I mentioned earlier in this book how your brain performs a risk assessment on all information that comes through your senses. If a perceived threat is present, your sympathetic nervous system will activate to protect you. Sometimes the threat is not a life-or-death issue. However, your ability to think decreases so your body can respond to the threat. This happens when you face something stressful, difficult, or unpleasant. If you face these sorts of things regularly, your body will move into a chronic state of dysfunction.[5] "Chronic dysregulation causes us to feel and act as if we're frozen in time, locked in an endless cycle of self-defeating behaviors that undermine us and distress those around us."[6] You have experienced this in your counseling sessions, in your staff meetings, in conflict, and in planning your calendar.

Rest isn't helpful at this time. Instead, it is your ability to practice self-regulation that will revitalize you. To do this, you must learn how to shift your attention away from everything demanding your attention and tune into your body. This is interoception. The goal is to notice and acknowledge your physical sensations.[7] Scan your body for signs of tension, noticing what parts are tight or rigid. It is purposeful activity amid the stressor and during the sympathetic arousal that is most important. While exercise and activity are helpful each day, those do not have the same positive effect as compared to self-regulation amid the stressor. You must

3. Chandler, "Pastoral Burnout," 283.
4. Csiernik and Adams, "Spirituality," 30.
5. Gentry and Block, *Forward Facing Trauma Therapy*, loc. 515.
6. Gentry and Block, *Forward Facing Trauma Therapy*, loc. 568.
7. Gentry and Block, *Forward Facing Trauma Therapy*, loc. 515.

integrate regulatory practices in your work throughout the day to be effective. It means paying attention to your physical responses, pausing to breathe, and doing momentary acts to calm yourself. To accomplish this, you must first be mindful.

Mindfulness can be a scary word for some. But it was a common practice for Jesus. Think of the moments when he stopped and paid attention. A wonderful example is the woman touching his cloak in the crowd. He asks, "Who touched me?" How did Jesus know someone had touched him in the midst of a group? He was mindful, and he felt power leave him.[8] Mindfulness is related to spiritual intelligence. It is the art of paying attention to your physical sensations, to what is happening around you, but not evaluating or judging it. The best synonym for mindfulness is noticing. It means staying in the present moment, not thinking of the future or the past. It's an alertness. Spiritual leaders who practice mindfulness experience lower levels of burnout, experience less stress, and report higher satisfaction in ministry.[9] The easiest way to begin is describing aloud what you hear, see, taste, touch, and feel in everyday activities like washing your hands. As you focus on the sensations, you move to a single-mindedness that relaxes and calms the nervous system. When you learn the art of mindfulness, you will notice a change in your perceptions of yourself and the world.

People who have burnout or compassion fatigue have a negative view of themselves and the world. As they struggle with confidence, they demand more of themselves to prove their competency, they work harder to accomplish more, and their self-esteem plummets.[10] This exacerbates the problem and needs a remedy. The practice of compassion, and specifically self-compassion, are powerful in reviving you. The practices of self-regulation and mindfulness increase compassion satisfaction and decrease burnout and compassion fatigue.[11] Self-compassion moves you from a

8. Luke 8:45.

9. Bloom, *Flourishing*, 20.

10. Gentry and Baranowsky, "Compassion Fatigue," 6.

11. Hotchkiss and Lesher, "Factors Predicting Burnout," 87.

failure mindset to a growth mindset even when facing perceived failures.[12] It is a recognition that you are created in God's image and bear those characteristics. Self-compassion restores your sense of worth in God's kingdom. "I liken this deepest dignity, this True Self who we are at our core, to a diamond buried deep within us and constantly forming under the intense pressure of our lives. We must search for and uncover this diamond, freeing it from the surrounding debris of guilt and shame. In a sense, our True Self must, like Jesus, be resurrected."[13]

When life is stressful, being self-compassionate means you treat yourself with kindness instead of judgment, that you recognize your humanity and how your response is common to other humans, and you bear sympathy for your pain. It's about seeing yourself through God's loving eyes. When you regain a sense of who you are in God's eyes, then you gain a wider view of humanity. It makes you more compassionate and forgiving of others. And it connects you to a community of support.

Create Connections

Connection with others who understand your dilemma is critical. You must build a support network that has your best interests in mind and yet is unafraid to practice honesty with you. These should be people who sing your praises and offer encouragement yet hold you accountable. This might be friends or family, the congregation, leaders of your faith group, and other pastors or spiritual mentors.

The congregation can be problematic, both a blessing and yet not helpful. Bloom says, "Pastors flourish when they feel they belong to this community—when they feel accepted, affirmed, and cared for by their local congregation—and their well-being is diminished when they feel in some way outside of the community."[14]

12. Cooke-Cottone and Guyker, "Development and Validation," 162.
13. Rohr, "Everything Is Grace," 1.
14. Bloom, *Flourishing*, 23.

As a leader, you need a community of believers who accept your humanness instead of expecting perfection, who grant you freedom to set boundaries around your personal life, and yet welcome you into fellowship, and who encourage you to be authentic. Your church system may provide this, but they need to know what you need to serve their mission best. This means you need to identify those things in the work system toxic to you. Which things are most challenging? How can you invite the church to walk alongside you, bearing the yoke with you?

You need an external support system, one that is unrelated to your work, to provide you with care. This works best when you find like-minded spiritual caregivers who are positive, responsive, and who offer you and one another mutual respect. Each bears his or her responsibility but engages in ways that offer support and encouragement to the others in the group.[15] It means entering intentional relationships or groups where everyone understands the value and importance of connection. It needs to be a group where you know you are not alone but part of something bigger, where members provide support in words and deeds, encourage genuine conversations, and notice the signs of burnout or stress and then act to offer help.[16]

You need a supportive family, who understand the stress you bear, and invite you to be fully present when home and engage you in joy-sustaining activities. And, you can support them by drawing boundaries and leaving the work at the door when possible, so family life revolves around relationships rather than your work environment. Then, you provide your family with loving care as part of your calling to ministry.

15. Bloom, *Flourishing*, 23.
16. Meek et al., "Maintaining Personal Resiliency," 343.

Reflection

This chapter mentioned the road to recovery is through intentionality, resiliency, and making connections. Try the following exercise to increase intentionality.

- Write out a mission statement. It should provide you with direction, purpose, and motivation. It should fit your personality and God's calling for your life. Let it describe your role as a minister, your vision, and what inspires you. Don't try to impress anyone. Write from your heart.

- Reread your mission statement. How does that fit your present ministry? What changes do you need to make?

- How can you set some boundaries to honor this mission statement? What plan can you develop to ensure you remain true to this mission?

Now that you've developed your mission statement, try the following exercises to increase self-regulation and build self-compassion:

- Close your eyes and with your mouth closed, allow a yawn to come upon you. Don't let it go so far that you actually yawn or open your mouth. Just let it grow inside your mouth and relax your jaw. What do you notice?

- Be still and use your senses. Describe what you see in detail. Then describe aloud what you hear. Move on to describe what you physically are touching, what you smell, and what you taste. Don't evaluate or judge it. Just describe it aloud. What changes do you notice? What happens to your stress?

- Place your hand on your heart. Think of someone you care about. Pray these words: May they receive peace. May they receive kindness. May they receive joy. Now think of someone with whom you've had a conflict and repeat the same words. Finally, keeping your hand on your heart, repeat the same prayer for yourself.

Practice all of these several times daily. Notice how your perspective changes. Finally, do this exercise to build connections. Make a list for the following:

- Who could I choose as a mentor or coach? Who is someone who could support and encourage me outside of my family?

- Is there a therapist, psychologist, or spiritual director who could help me? What do I need in order to ask for help?

- When can I plan time to retreat?

- How could I find a support group?

Now write a letter to yourself. This is the letter from an admired mentor. The letter can only say good, kind, and caring things. It should focus on your strengths and accomplishments. Once you've written the letter, read it aloud to yourself. Then save the letter to read when you begin to experience doubt.

"Men and women are called to enduring hope. True hope is not based on the ebb and flow of our feelings. Nor does it come from success in life. True hope—which means the hope that endures and sustains us—is based on God's call and command."[17]

17. Moltmann, *Experience of God*, 9.

Chapter 11

Share the Buoys

And should I not have concern for the great city of Nineveh,
in which there are more than a hundred and twenty thousand
people who cannot tell their right hand from their left—
and also many animals?

—JONAH 4:11

Do you find it odd that the last verse in the book of Jonah ends
with a question from God? I do not know the rest of the story. It's
God's response to Jonah's anger. It's a rhetorical question with an
obvious answer, intending to tell Jonah that God's redemption is
of utmost importance. It's also a reminder that the world does not
revolve around Jonah, his desires, and his personal needs. There is
something far larger that concerns God—the needs of all the people.

When you are experiencing burnout or compassion fatigue,
or emotional exhaustion, or weariness, despair or loneliness, you
become self-focused. It's natural. If you stub your toe, it's difficult to
think about anything but your pain. If you lose someone you love,
your world stops while you mourn. But there are people around
you who are crying. They weep for lost dreams, feel discouraged
by the ministry, and are hanging on by a thread. Some are clergy

spouses, clergy children, lay leaders, or other pastoral caregivers. God's heart is for those who are brokenhearted.

There is a great deal of pressure on the minister's family, especially in church settings. Most of the stressors center on expectations and boundaries. In a study of clergy children in adulthood, many reported their experience as a "PK," pastor's kid. While expected to endure difficulties without complaint, clergy children were also called upon to set examples for other children and teens in the congregation.[1] "You are a minister's child, you represent all youth. There is always scrutiny about what pastors' children do and do not do."[2] This is setting the bar higher for them than their peers, and yet their needs are like their friends. The adult clergy children also reported the lack of privacy they experienced, as any activity observed by either peers or other adults were often relayed to their parents and throughout the congregation.[3] Another dilemma faced by clergy children was critique about their choices, their appearance, and their parents. Church members treat clergy children as mini adults, expecting the maturity of an adult in a child or adolescent. Clergy children listening to their parents' recollections of church members also had a negative impact, creating lower life satisfaction in adolescence.[4]

Pastors and churches have a shared responsibility in providing clergy children with the support they need. By allowing privacy and changing expectations, these children need to develop in the same manner their peers grow. Church members can offer protection to clergy children by refusing to take part in discussions or critiques and instead relaying the message that these children need normal lives. Also, church members should refrain from expressing thoughts or feelings about the minister's performance to family members. Those conversations should remain between the parishioner and the leader. I remind congregants that they likely would be averse to hearing their employees or fellow coworkers relay gossip

1. Wilson and Darling, "Understanding Stress," 130.
2. Hill et al., "Understanding Boundary-Related Stress," 159.
3. Wilson and Darling, "Understanding Stress," 130.
4. Wilson and Darling, "Understanding Stress," 139.

or criticism about their own children. In addition, pastors and their spouses can offer their children freedom to be themselves.

Clergy spouses experience the same difficulty with unrealistic expectations and boundary violations. It's difficult to set the privacy and space needed to separate the family from the church. Clergy spouses struggle with the lack of privacy and the constant criticism, often feeling as if they live in a glass house. It's difficult to know how to deal with the intrusion. However, compared to the minister, the clergy spouses are more affected by the stressors, experience more negative thoughts, and have fewer coping resources.[5] Here's Amanda's story:

> We live in a fishbowl. Everything we do or say is repeated and judged. I hear someone say, "People are wondering why your children aren't wearing dress clothes to church." Or they offer advice, "Do you really think it's okay to take a vacation now?" Popping by my house, they expect I have a magic cake prepared to serve with a high-quality coffee. "Why aren't you teaching Sunday school?" "You know, our former pastor's wife played the piano." Or they make comments about my looks. "Oh, dear, here's the number for my hairdresser. She could help you with your hair." "Are you feeling okay, you always look so tired?" Even worse, they feel it is okay to tell me my husband's faults. "You know, he really isn't Billy Graham." "Have you noticed he has difficulty reading?" "He can't seem to get a handle, can he?" I want to tell them what I think of their children, their appearance, their husband, but I can't. I am the pastor's wife, after all. My job is to remain poised, no matter what. Yet watching my husband grow more discouraged, listening to stories of conflict, and unending criticism makes me wonder how I ended up here.

It's the ambiguity of how and when to set those boundaries that leaves clergy families confused. The spouses remark how the minister is on call every day and interruptions to family time are common. Sometimes frequent moves interfere with developing

---

5. Darling et al., "Understanding Stress and Quality," 263.

helpful outside support.[6] It's difficult for clergy spouses to find their own identity and space, besides protecting their family. This is problematic when living in a parsonage.[7] Add to this, the pastor who is sharing his or her frustrations with the church, needing support from his or her spouse, yet not always ensuring his or her spouse have the coping resources needed.

Clergy husbands experience similar dilemmas to clergy wives and yet have some unique struggles. For some clergy husbands, they feel they are second to their wives' calling to ministry and their roles are more ambiguous in the church setting.[8] Clergy husbands typically choose one of three roles: team worker, background supporter, or aloof participant.[9] There is still little written about the clergy wife and supporting husband that needs exploration. Possibly those couples can bring light to managing clergy families and their relationship to church systems.

There are primarily five types of personal care that benefit ministry spouses: spiritual disciplines and connection with God, shared calling in ministry, private engagement with one's spouse, time away from the ministry setting, and supportive friendships.[10] Spouses can also develop personal coping resources such as personal time with God, developing self-esteem and self-compassion, and creating a flexible role for themselves. Spouses fare better when they have a shared calling and vision for the ministry.[11] Enhancing the marital relationship heightens satisfaction in ministry, but the minister and spouse must be intentional in their efforts to spend time together. In addition, finding time away from the ministry setting is helpful. While ministers have access to outside support, it's more difficult for their spouses to find a community of friends. This results in feeling isolated.[12] Finding a support network is vital.

6. Hill et al., "Understanding Boundary-Related Stress," 155.

7. Hill et al., "Understanding Boundary-Related Stress," 155.

8. Aulthouse, "Clergy Families," 6.

9. Aulthouse, "Clergy Families," 6.

10. McMinn et al., "Care for Pastors," 575–77.

11. Luedtke and Sneed, "Voice of the Clergy Wife," 66–67.

12. Hill et al., "Understanding Boundary-Related Stress," 157.

Spiritual resources are necessary for the clergy family. Whenever adequate tools are at hand, then happiness, compassion, and satisfaction increase. It is common when ministers suffer from burnout or compassion fatigue, their spouses share in that distress, even when not directly involved in the care of others.[13] Clergy families could benefit from ongoing denominational or faith group support that provide education and enrichment programs that address the well-being of their families. Offering opportunities for connection for minister spouses would be helpful. For clergy spouses who are experiencing burnout or compassion fatigue, the recommendations in this book serve as the foundation for recovery.

Reflection

This chapter mentions the way in which clergy spouses and clergy children struggle. Consider the following questions:

1. In what way does your family struggle (boundaries, frequent moves, financial, expectations)?

2. How can you establish clear boundaries and yet continue to support the mission?

3. What would "normal" family life mean to you?

4. Who best supports your family?

5. In what ways do your children struggle or have your children struggled? How can you help them?

When I remember who I serve—God—and to whom I minister—people who have lost their courage or hope, then I can say, "It's really worth all the trouble." This wonderful, beautiful, frustrating, demanding thing isn't just a job. It's a calling. I'm are chosen to be God's presence to a hurting world. That is such an honor.

13. Darling et al., "Understanding Stress and Quality," 272.

Chapter 12

Swim with Friends

From inside the fish Jonah prayed to the Lord his God. He said:
"In my distress I called to the Lord, and he answered me. From deep
in the realm of the dead I called for help, and you listened to my cry.
. . . When my life was ebbing away, I remembered you, Lord, and my
prayer rose to you, to your holy temple. Those who cling to worthless
idols turn away from God's love for them. But I, with shouts of
grateful praise, will sacrifice to you. What I have vowed I will make
good. I will say, 'Salvation comes from the Lord.'" And the Lord
commanded the fish, and it vomited Jonah onto dry land.

—JONAH 2:1–2, 7–9

YOU ARE NOT ALONE. You are one of many pastors, ministry leaders, clergy, chaplains, counselors, or volunteer leaders who work
for God. The Holy One hears your prayer. God's heart breaks for
you in your struggle to do God's will. While it seems as if you swim
alone, you do not. You are surrounded by those who've done this
before and who will do it after you leave ministry. Elijah thought
he was alone. God reminded him that there were seven thousand

who worshipped God, and that Elijah's mission was not complete.[1] God was telling Elijah to finish the job.

When you are hurt by your people, and your followers are hard-headed, then it is hard to keep on loving them. Your compassion wanes, and you detach. It's how you protect yourself. You don't want to feel mercy because it opens your wounds. You're worn out. But the Lord calls you back to the people. God shows a different way. Larry Crabb says, "Out of his great love, God has taken it upon himself to reconnect us, first to himself by revealing that he is that good; then to ourselves and others by pouring his goodness into our hearts, a goodness that enables us to live with integrity, prompted by spiritual dynamics, and aware of urges within us to bless others."[2] God places within you, at your spiritual new birth, goodness, a likeness of the Holy One that draws you to the Divine and to one another. That goodness helps you see yourself and people, not for their faults or their difficult temperaments, but as humans with great potential whom you can guide in Christian love. It is that renewed vision that allows you to recommit to the people of God.[3] "We love because he first loved us."[4]

You may think you've failed, and perhaps some view it that way. Jesus was a failure to some. The Jews needed someone to free them from the tyranny of the Roman government. They wanted liberty to practice their religion and possess their rightful inheritance of the surrounding land. When Jesus arrived on the scene with the declaration that he was the Messiah, the fervor swelled. The crowds followed. Speaking with authority, Jesus brought a fresh teaching to the torah and healing. He gave hope and freedom to the oppressed. But he failed. He didn't overthrow the Romans. He didn't become the king of the Jews. His followers deserted him and even his closest friends and allies betrayed him. Jesus failed. But did he?

---

1. 1 Kgs 19:18.
2. Crabb, *Connecting*, 18–19.
3. Hoppe, "Self-Directed Approach," 182.
4. 1 John 4:19.

And when Jesus had cried out again in a loud voice, he
gave up his spirit. At that moment the curtain of the temple was torn in two from top to bottom. The earth shook,
the rocks split and the tombs broke open. The bodies of
many holy people who had died were raised to life. They
came out of the tombs after Jesus' resurrection and went
into the holy city and appeared to many people. When
the centurion and those with him were guarding Jesus
saw the earthquake and all that had happened, they were
terrified, and exclaimed, "Sure he was the Son of God."[5]

Jesus disappointed the world. In this moment of his death,
only a few could see his true nature. Jesus could not have done
this without his calling and confidence. He claimed God's vision as
his own. "Jesus knew that the Father had put all things under his
power, and that he had come from God and was returning to God;
he got up from the meal, took off his outer clothing, and wrapped
a towel around his waist. After that, he poured water into a basin
and began to wash his disciples' feet, drying them with the towel
that was wrapped around him."[6] Despite knowing the pain he
would face, and knowing he would be betrayed by all the disciples,
Jesus humbled himself to service for the sake of the kingdom.

God calls you to be the physical and emotional presence of
the sacred in the world. You are a wounded healer. Out of the pain
you experience comes the ability to care more deeply. Empathy
increases and you engage with others. Viktor Frankl says, "Suffering ceases to be suffering in some way at the moment it finds a
meaning."[7] The pain you endure comes from the ministry you
offer. Louw says this is the role of pastoral care and it emerges
from the suffering of Christ and comfort from God.[8] It is the opportunity to be fully present with those in pain, to bridge the gap
between a fallen world and the kingdom of God, to offer unconditional love, while providing hope for the future. Your failure is

5. Matt 27:50–54.

6. John 13:3–5.

7. Frankl, *Man's Search for Meaning*, 115.

8. Louw, "Compassion," 8.

temporary but represents a "yearning for wholeness" that comes only by focusing on the larger picture of redemption.[9] In your call, you can speak for the voiceless, cry out for those who are hopeless, and show them the way home. Swim with them. They need you. Swim with friends.

9. Louw, "Compassion," 9.

Bibliography

Aaker, Dane. "The Church Bizarre." CT Pastors. *Leadership Journal,* September 13, 2016. https://www.christianitytoday.com/pastors/2000/winter/14.85.html.

Abernethy, Alexis D., et al. "The Pastors Empowerment Program: A Resilience Education Intervention to Prevent Clergy Burnout." *Spirituality in Clinical Practice* 3 (2016) 175–86. https://doi.org/10.1037/scp0000109.

Adelstein, Pamela. "Sacred Space." *Global Advances in Health and Medicine* 7 (2018) 1–2. https://doi.org/10.1177/2164957X17751903.

Alarcon, Gene, et al. "Relationships between Personality Variables and Burnout: A Meta-Analysis." *Work & Stress* 23 (2009) 244–63. https://doi.org/10.1080/02678370903282600.

Alessandri, Guido, et al. "Job Burnout: The Contribution of Emotional Stability and Emotional Self-Efficacy Beliefs." *Journal of Occupational and Organizational Psychology* 91 (2018) 823–51. https://doi.org/10.1111/joop.12225.

Allen, Blaine. *Before You Quit: When Ministry Is Not What You Thought.* Grand Rapids: Kregel, 2001.

American Red Cross. "Water Safety." RedCross.org. https://www.redcross.org/get-help/how-to-prepare-for-emergencies/types-of-emergencies/water-safety.html.

Armour, Michael C., and Don Browning. *Systems-Sensitive Leadership: Empowering Diversity without Polarizing the Church.* Joplin, MO: College Press, 2000.

Associated Press. "Fran Crippen Dies in Open-Water Event." *ESPN.com,* October 23, 2010. https://www.espn.com/olympics/swimming/news/story?id=5718372.

Aulthouse, Michelle E. "Clergy Families: The Helpless Forgottens' Cry for Help Answered through Reality Therapy." *VISTAS Online.* Article 47. Paper based on program presented at the American Counseling Association Conference, Cincinnati, March 20–24, 2013. https://www.counseling.org/docs/default-source/vistas/clergy-families-the-helpless-forgottens-cry-for-help.pdf?sfvrsn=1c17cd2b_11.

Bibliography

Bancewicz, Ruth M. "In the Eye of the Barracuda: Beauty in the Ocean." *Science and Belief*, May 28, 2015. https://scienceandbelief.org/2015/05/28/in-the-eye-of-the-barracuda-beauty-in-the-ocean/.

Barnard, Laura K., and John F. Curry. "The Relationship of Clergy Burnout to Self-Compassion and Other Personality Dimensions." *Pastoral Psychology* 61 (2012) 149–63. https://link.springer.com/article/10.1007/s11089-011-0377-0.

Baxter, Richard. *The Reformed Pastor*. Richmond, VA: John Knox, 1956.

Baylor University. "Seminaries Do Very Little to Train Pastors How to Help Mentally Ill Congregants, Baylor Study Finds." Media and Public Relations, Baylor University, September 8, 2014. https://www.baylor.edu/mediacommunications/news.php?action=story&story=146178.

Bester, Cathleen. "Sphyraena Barracuda." Florida Museum, May 12, 2017. https://www.floridamuseum.ufl.edu/discover-fish/species-profiles/sphyraena-barracuda/.

Bettis, Kara. "The 4 Great Challenges of Christian Counseling." CT Pastors. *Christianity Today*, February 7, 2018. https://www.christianitytoday.com/pastors/2018/february-web-exclusives/4-great-challenges-of-christian-counseling.html.

Bickerton, Grant. "Well-Being in Ministry Results Overview." *University of Western Sydney*. https://www.buv.com.au/documents/item/182.

Bishop, Kelly Ladd. "I Was Betrayed by the Church and Here's What I Learned." *Missio Alliance*, April 6, 2017. https://www.missioalliance.org/betrayed-church-heres-learned/.

Bixby, Douglas J. *Navigating the Nonsense: Church Conflict and Triangulation*. Eugene, OR: Cascade, 2016.

Bloom, Matt. *Flourishing in Ministry: Emerging Research Insights on the Well-Being of Pastors*. Mendoza College of Business, University of Notre Dame, 2013. https://wellbeing.nd.edu/assets/198819/emerging_insights_2_1_.pdf.

Bond, Daisy, et al. "The Association between Anthropometric Variables, Functional Movement Screen Scores and 100 m Freestyle Swimming Performance in Youth Swimmers." *Sports* 3 (2015) 1–11. https://doi.org/10.3390/sports3010001.

Cavanaugh, Brian, ed. *More Sower's Seeds: Second Planting*. Mahwah, NJ: Paulist, 1992.

Chandy, Dipak, and Gerald L. Weinhouse. "Drowning (Submersion Injuries)." *UpToDate*, January 21, 2020. https://www.uptodate.com/contents/drowning-submersion-injuries.

Charry, Ellen T. *By the Renewing of Your Minds: The Pastoral Function of Christian Doctrine*. New York: Oxford University Press, 1997.

Childs, Brevard S. *The Book of Exodus*. Philadelphia: Westminster, 1974.

Cook-Cottone, et al. "The Development and Validation of the Mindful Self-Care Scale (MSCS): An Assessment of Practices That Support Positive Embodiment." *Mindfulness* 9 (2018) 161–75. https://link.springer.com/article/10.1007/s12671-017-0759-1.

Bibliography

Crabb, Larry. *Connecting: Healing for Ourselves and Our Relationship—a Radical New Vision*. Nashville: Word, 1997.

Csiernik, Rick, and David Adams. "Spirituality, Stress and Work." *Employee Assistance Quarterly* 18 (2002) 29–37. https://doi.org/10.1300/J022v18n02_02.

Csikszentmihalyi, Mihaly. *Flow: The Psychology of Optimal Experience*. New York: Harper & Row, 1990.

Darling, Carol Anderson, et al. "Understanding Stress and Quality of Life for Clergy and Clergy Spouses." *Stress and Health* 20 (2004) 261–77. https://onlinelibrary.wiley.com/doi/abs/10.1002/smi.1031.

Dawn, Marva, and Eugene Peterson. *The Unnecessary Pastor: Rediscovering the Call*. Grand Rapids: Eerdmans, 2000.

Donovan, Matt. "How to Fix Common Breathing Mistakes in Swimming." *U.S. Masters Swimming*, October 24, 2019. https://www.usms.org/fitness-and-training/articles-and-videos/articles/how-to-fix-common-breathing-mistakes-in-swimming.

Doolittle, Benjamin R. "Burnout and Coping among Parish-Based Clergy." *Mental Health, Religion & Culture* 10 (2007) 31–38. https://doi.org/10.1080/13674670600857591.

Farrell, Jennifer L., and Deborah A. Goebert. "Collaboration between Psychiatrists and Clergy in Recognizing and Treating Serious Mental Illness." *Psychiatric Services* 59 (2008) 437–40. https://doi.org/10.1176/ps.2008.59.4.437.

Field, Bob. "Falling Apart in Christian Ministry." *Pointers: Bulletin of the Christian Research Association* 27 (June 2017) 11–13. https://search.informit.org/documentSummary;dn=887803625299391;res=IELHSS.

Figley, Charles R. *Compassion Fatigue: Coping with Secondary Traumatic Stress Disorder in Those Who Treat the Traumatized*. New York: Routledge, 1995.

Fletemeyer, John R. "What Really Happens When Someone Drowns." https://www.aquaticsintl.com/lifeguards/what-really-happens-when-someone-drowns_o.

Francis, Leslie, et al. "Work-Related Psychological Wellbeing: Testing the Balanced Affect Model among Anglican Clergy." *Religions* 8 (2017) 1–11. https://doi.org/10.3390/rel8070118.

Frankl, Viktor Emil. *Man's Search for Meaning: An Introduction to Logotherapy*. Translated by Ilse Lasch. New York: Simon & Schuster, 1959.

Fray, Harold R. *The Pain and Joy of Ministry*. Philadelphia: Pilgrim, 1972.

Freudenberger, Herbert J., and Geraldine Richelson. *Burn-Out: The High Cost of High Achievement*. Garden City: Anchor, 1980.

Friedman, Edwin H. *Generation to Generation: Family Process in Church and Synagogue*. New York: Guilford, 2011.

Gaal, Marty. "Proper Breathing Technique for Swimming." *Active*. https://www.active.com/triathlon/articles/proper-breathing-technique-for-swimming-875008.

Bibliography

Gentry, J. Eric, and Anna B. Baranowsky. "Compassion Fatigue Resiliency—a New Attitude." 2013. http://psychink.com/ticlearn/wp-content/uploads/2013/10/Compassion-Resiliency-A-New-Attitude.pdf.

Gentry, J. Eric, and Ilisa Keith Block. *Forward Facing Trauma Therapy: Healing the Moral Wound.* Sarasota, FL: Compassion Unlimited, 2016.

Grosch, William N., and David C. Olsen. "Clergy Burnout: An Integrative Approach." *Journal of Clinical Psychology* 56 (2000) 619–32. https://doi.org/10.1002/(sici)1097-4679(200005)56:5<619::aid-jclp4>3.0.co;2-2.

Hendron, Jill Anne, et al. "The Unseen Cost: A Discussion of the Secondary Traumatization Experience of the Clergy." *Pastoral Psychology* 61 (2012) 221–31. https://link.springer.com/article/10.1007/s11089-011-0378-z.

Hill, E. Wayne, et al. "Understanding Boundary-Related Stress in Clergy Families." *Marriage & Family Review* 35 (2003) 147–66. https://doilorg/10.1300/J002v35n01_09.

Hoppe, Kathy. "A Self-Directed Approach to the Treatment of Burnout in Pastors." DMin. thesis, Oral Roberts University, 2003.

Hotchkiss, Jason T., and Ruth Lesher. "Factors Predicting Burnout among Chaplains: Compassion Satisfaction, Organizational Factors, and the Mediators of Mindful Self-Care and Secondary Traumatic Stress." *Journal of Pastoral Care & Counseling* 72 (2018) 86–98. https://doi.org/10.1177/1542305018780655.

Hula, Ed, III. "Fran Crippen Report Demands Major Changes for Marathon Swim." *AroundtheRings,* April 18, 2011. http://aroundtherings.com/site/A__36832/Title__Fran-Crippen-Report-Demands-Major-Changes-for-Marathon-Swim/292/Articles.

Hulme, William E. *Managing Stress in Ministry.* San Francisco: Harper & Row, 1985.

Jackson-Jordan, Elizabeth Ann. "Clergy Burnout and Resilience: A Review of the Literature." *Journal of Pastoral Care & Counseling* 67 (February 2013) 1–6. http://dx.doi.org/10.1177/154230501306700103.

Jacobson, Jodi M., et al. "Risk for Burnout and Compassion Fatigue and Potential for Compassion Satisfaction among Clergy: Implications for Social Work and Religious Organizations." *Journal of Social Service Research* 39 (2013) 455–68. https://doi.org/10.1080/01488376.2012.744627.

Joinson, Carla. "Coping with Compassion Fatigue." *Nursing* 22 (April 1992) 116–21. https://doi.org/10.1097/00152193-199204000-00035.

Jowett, John. *The Preacher, His Life and Work.* Grand Rapids: Baker, 1968.

Kempis, Thomas à. *The Imitation of Christ.* Fairfield, IA: 1st World Library, 2004.

Kerr, Michael E. *One Family's Story: A Primer on Bowen Theory.* Washington, DC: Bowen Center for the Study of the Family, Georgetown Family Center, 2003.

Kerr, Michael E., and Murray Bowen. *Family Evaluation: An Approach Based on Bowen Theory.* New York: Norton, 1988.

Bibliography

Kostich, Alex. "Simple Techniques for Swimming Straight in Open Water." *Active. com.* https://www.active.com/articles/simple-techniques-for-swimming -straight-in-open-water?page=1.

Krejcir, Richard J. "Statistics on Pastors." *Into Thy Word: Teaching People How to Study the Bible* (blog). 2007. http://www.intothyword.org/apps/ articles/?articleid=36562.

LaMothe, Ryan. "Broken and Empty: Pastoral Leadership as Embodying Radical Courage, Humility, Compassion, and Hope." *Pastoral Psychology* 61 (2012) 451–66. https://www.researchgate.net/publication/257635490_ Broken_and_Empty_Pastoral_Leadership_as_Embodying_Radical_ Courage_Humility_Compassion_and_Hope.

Lloyd, Tony. "Climate Stories: What I Learned by Nearly Drowning." *Climate Reality,* January 2, 2020. https://climaterealityproject.org/blog/climate- stories-what-i-learned-nearly-drowning.

Louw, Daniël. "Compassion Fatigue: Spiritual Exhaustion and the Cost of Caring in the Pastoral Ministry: Towards a 'Pastoral Diagnosis' in Caregiving." *HTS Teologiese Studies/Theological Studies* 71 (June 2015) 1–10. https://doi.org/10.4102/hts.v71i2.3032.

Luedtke, Amy C., and Katti J. Sneed. "Voice of the Clergy Wife: A Phenomenological Study." *Journal of Pastoral Care & Counseling* 72 (2018) 63–72. https://doi.org/10.1177/1542305018762212.

Maslach, Christina. "Finding Solutions to the Problem of Burnout." *Consulting Psychology Journal: Practice and Research* 69 (2017) 143–52. http://dx.doi. org/10.1037/cpb0000090.

Maslach, Christina, and Michael P. Leiter. "Latent Burnout Profiles: A New Approach to Understanding the Burnout Experience." *Burnout Research* 3 (September 2016) 89–100. https://dx.doi.org/10.1016/j.burn.2016.09.001.

———. "Understanding the Burnout Experience: Recent Research and Its Implications for Psychiatry." *World Psychiatry* 15 (June 2016) 103–11. https://doi.org/10.1002/wps.20311.

McBurney, Louis. *Every Pastor Needs a Pastor.* Waco, TX: Word, 1977.

McMinn, Mark R., et al. "Care for Pastors: Learning From Clergy and Their Spouses." *Pastoral Psychology* 53 (2005) 563–81. https://digitalcommons. georgefox.edu/cgi/viewcontent.cgi?article=1197&context=gscp_fac.

Meek, Katheryn Rhoads, et al. "Maintaining Personal Resiliency: Lessons Learned from Evangelical Protestant Clergy." *Journal of Psychology and Theology* 31 (December 2003) 339–47. http://dx.doi. org/10.1177/009164710303100404.

Miller, Brian, and Ginny Sprang. "A Components-Based Practice and Supervision Model for Reducing Compassion Fatigue by Affecting Clinician Experience." *Traumatology* 23 (January 2016) 153–64. https:// doi.org/10.1037/trm0000058.

Moltmann, Jurgen. *Experience of God.* Philadelphia: Fortress, 1980.

Bibliography

Mortenson, J. P. "What Makes the Perfect Swimmer's Body?" *Swimming World*, August 19, 2020. https://www.swimmingworldmagazine.com/news/what-makes-the-perfect-swimmers-body.

Muller, Wayne. *Sabbath: Restoring the Sacred Rhythm of Rest*. New York: Bantam, 1999.

NCLS Research. "Personal Foundations." Leadership: Information for Church Leaders. *NCLS.org*. http://www.ncls.org.au/default.aspx?sitemapid=6975.

Nessan, Craig L. "Surviving Congregational Leadership: A Theology of Family Systems." *Congregation* 20 (2005) 390–99. https://www.semanticscholar.org/paper/Surviving-Congregational-Leadership-:-A-Theology-of-Nessan/363d6830ea62168b983278a2bafe2af2e72eee4a.

New Zealand Ocean Swim Series. "Ocean Swimming Navigation Tips." OceanSwim.co.nz, April 2, 2013. https://oceanswim.co.nz/ocean-swimming-navigation-tips/.

Nichols, Scott. "Pastors & Burnout: A Personal Reflection." *ChristianityToday*, November 22, 2019. https://www.christianitytoday.com/edstetzer/2019/november/pastors-burnout-personal-reflection.html.

Noullet, Christopher J., et al. "Effect of Pastoral Crisis Intervention Training on Resilience and Compassion Fatigue in Clergy: A Pilot Study." *Spirituality in Clinical Practice* 5 (2018) 1–7. https://doi.org/10.1037/scp0000158.

Nouwen, Henri J. *The Way of the Heart*. New York: Seabury, 1981.

Odom, David L. "Dave Odom: The Path to Increased Pastoral Agency." *Faith & Leadership*, May 14, 2019. https://faithandleadership.com/dave-odom-path-increased-pastoral-agency.

Oswald, Roy M. "How Dry Is Your Well? A Burnout Self-Assessment Tool." Quiet Waters Ministries. https://www.qwaters.org/wp-content/uploads/2016/12/Burnout-Survey.pdf.

Poirier-Leroy, Olivier. "Beginner's Guide to Open Water Swimming Gear." *Your Swim Book*. https://www.yourswimlog.com/open-water-swimming-gear/.

Rainer, Thom S. "The Dangerous Third Year of Pastoral Tenure." ThomRainer.com (blog), June 18, 2014. https://thomrainer.com/2014/06/dangerous-third-year-pastoral-tenure/.

———. "Seven Reasons Why Many Pastors Avoid a Counseling Ministry." ThomRainer.com (blog), October 22, 2018. https://thomrainer.com/2018/10/seven-reasons-many-pastors-avoid-counseling-ministry/.

Ramani, Subha, et al. "Uncovering the Unknown: A Grounded Theory Study Exploring the Impact of Self-Awareness on the Culture of Feedback in Residency Education." *Medical Teacher* 39 (2017) 1065–73. https://doi.org/10.1080/0142159X.2017.1353071.

Randall, Kelvin J. "Clergy Burnout: Two Different Measures." *Pastoral Psychology* 62 (2013) 333–41. https://link.springer.com/article/10.1007/s11089-012-0506-4.

———. "Examining the Relationship between Burnout and Age among Anglican Clergy in England and Wales." *Mental Health, Religion and Culture* 10 (2007) 39–46. https://doi.org/10.1080/13674670601012303.

Bibliography

Reeves, Kenneth. *The Whole Church: Congregational Leadership Guided by Systems Theory.* Lanham, MD: Rowman & Littlefield, 2019.

Rios, Jaime. "I Was Seconds Away from Drowning in My Own Car—Until I Did This to Survive." *Reader's Digest,* updated February 2017. https://www.rd.com/advice/pets/survived-a-drowning/.

Rohr, Richard. "Everything Is Grace." *Center for Action and Contemplation,* February 5, 2016. https://cac.org/everything-is-grace-2016-02-05/.

———. "Trust the River." *Center for Action and Contemplation,* February 4, 2016. https://cac.org/trust-the-river-2016-02-04/.

Ross, Halle E., and Matthew S. Stanford. "Training and Education of North American Master's of Divinity Students in Relation to Serious Mental Illness." *Journal of Research in Christian Education* 23 (2014) 176–86. https://doi.org/10.1080/10656219.2014.899480.

Salwen, Erik D., et al. "Self-Disclosure and Spiritual Well-Being in Pastors Seeking Professional Psychological Help." *Pastoral Psychology* 66 (August 2017) 505–21. https://www.researchgate.net/publication/315886141_Self-Disclosure_and_Spiritual_Well-Being_in_Pastors_Seeking_Professional_Psychological_Help.

Sanford, John. *Ministry Burnout.* Louisville: Westminster, 1982.

Schnase, Robert. *Testing and Reclaiming Your Call to Ministry.* Nashville: Abingdon, 1991.

Scots College. "The Five Crucial Functions of Pastoral Care." The Scots College, Sydney, Australia. https://www.tsc.nsw.edu.au/tscnews/the-five-crucial-functions-of-pastoral-care.

Seymour, Jody. *A Time for Healing: Overcoming the Perils of Ministry.* Valley Forge, PA: Judson, 1995.

Sharma, Anita, and Neelabh Kashyap. "The Influence of the Big Five Personality Traits on Burnout in Medical Doctors." *International Journal of Psychological Studies* 9 (October 2017) 13–23. https://doi.org/10.5539/ijps.v9n4p13.

Siebert, Al. "Develop Resiliency Skills." *T + D* 60 (September 2006) 88–89.

Snelgar, Robin John, et al. "Preventing Compassion Fatigue amongst Pastors: The Influence of Spiritual Intelligence and Intrinsic Motivation." *Journal of Psychology and Theology* 45 (2017) 247–60. https://doi.org/10.1177/009164711704500401.

Sorenson, Claire, et al. "Understanding Compassion Fatigue in Healthcare Providers: A Review of Current Literature." *Journal of Nursing Scholarship* 48 (September 2016) 456–65. https://doi.org/10.1111/jnu.12229.

Spaite, Daniel, and Debbie Salter Goodwin. *Time Bomb in the Church.* Kansas City: Beacon Hill, 1999.

Spencer, J. Louis, et al. "Predicting the Level of Pastors' Risk of Termination/Exit from the Church." *Pastoral Psychology* 61 (2011) 85–98. https://www.researchgate.net/publication/257635485_Predicting_the_Level_of_Pastors%27_Risk_of_TerminationExit_from_the_Church.

Bibliography

Spurgeon, Charles H. *An All Round Ministry*. Edinburgh: Banner of Truth Trust, 1900.

Stamm, Beth Hudnall. *The Concise ProQOL Manual*. 2nd ed. Pocatello, ID: ProQOL.org, 2010.

———. "The Professional Quality of Life Scale (ProQOL)." https://www.proqol.org/uploads/ProQOL_5_English_Self-Score.pdf.

Steinke, Peter L. *Congregational Leadership in Anxious Times: Being Calm and Courageous No Matter What*. Lanham, MD: Rowman & Littlefield, 2006.

———. *Healthy Congregations: A Systems Approach*. Lanham, MD: Rowman & Littlefield, 2014.

———. *How Your Church Family Works: Understanding Congregations as Emotional Systems*. New York: Alban Institute, 1993.

Stevens, R. Paul., and Phil Collins. *The Equipping Pastor: A Systems Approach to Congregational Leadership*. Washington, DC: Alban Institute, 2000.

Thomas, Curtis C. *Practical Wisdom for Pastors*. Wheaton, IL: Crossway, 2001.

Tidball, Derek. *Skillful Shepherds: An Introduction to Pastoral Theology*. Philadelphia: Scribner, 1907.

Upadyaya, Katya, et al. "From Job Demands and Resources to Work Engagement, Burnout, Life Satisfaction, Depressive Symptoms, and Occupational Health." *Burnout Research* 3 (December 2016) 101–8. https://doi.org/10.1016/j.burn.2016.10.001.

Visker, Joseph D., et al. "Ministry-Related Burnout and Stress Coping Mechanisms among Assemblies of God–Ordained Clergy in Minnesota." *Journal of Religion and Health* 56 (August 2016) 951–61. https://www.researchgate.net/publication/306041220_Ministry-Related_Burnout_and_Stress_Coping_Mechanisms_Among_Assemblies_of_God-Ordained_Clergy_in_Minnesota.

Vittone, Mario, and Francesco A. Pia. "'It Doesn't Look Like They're Drowning': How to Recognize the Instinctive Drowning Response." *On Scene: The Journal of U. S. Coast Guard Search and Rescue* (Fall 2006) 14–16. http://mariovittone.com/wp-content/uploads/2010/05/OSFall06.pdf.

Von Schlichten, David. "The Pastoral Mystique: A Feminist Ecclesiological Approach to Clergy Burnout." *Journal of Moral Theology* 9 (2020) 190–202. https://jmt.scholasticahq.com/article/11611-the-pastoral-mystique-a-feminist-ecclesiological-approach-to-clergy-burnout.

Vu, Francis, and Patrick Bodenmann. "Preventing, Managing and Treating Compassion Fatigue." *Swiss Archives of Neurology, Psychiatry and Psychotherapy* 168 (2017) 224–31. https://doi.org/10.4414/sanp.2017.00525.

Watson, Kathryn. "Drowning Facts and Safety Precautions." *Healthline*, March 24, 2020. https://www.healthline.com/health/how-long-does-it-take-to-drown.

Weaver, Andrew J., et al. "Collaboration between Clergy and Mental Health Professionals: A Review of Professional Health Care Journals from 1980 through 1999." *Counseling and Values* 47 (2003) 162–71. https://onlinelibrary.wiley.com/doi/abs/10.1002/j.2161-007X.2003.tb00263.x.

Bibliography

Wiener, Aharon. *The Prophet Elijah in the Development of Judaism: A Depth-Psychological Study.* London: Routledge & Kegan Paul, 1978.

Willimon, William H. *Clergy and Laity Burnout.* Nashville: Abingdon, 1989.

Wilson, Cynthia B., and Carol Anderson Darling. "Understanding Stress and Life Satisfaction for Children of Clergy: A Retrospective Study." *Pastoral Psychology* 66 (2017) 129–42. https://link.springer.com/article/10.1007/s11089-016-0720-6.

Wilson, Jacque. "Water Safety Expert: 'Drowning Doesn't Just Happen.'" *CNN.com*, March 14, 2013. https://www.cnn.com/2013/03/13/health/adolescent-pool-safety/index.html.

World Health Organization. "Drowning." WHO, Fact Sheets, February 3, 2020. https://www.who.int/news-room/fact-sheets/detail/drowning.

Zapf, Dieter. "Emotion Work and Psychological Well-Being: A Review of the Literature and Some Conceptual Considerations." *Human Resource Management Review* 12 (December 2001) 237–68. https://www.sciencedirect.com/science/article/abs/pii/S1053482202000487?via%3Dihub.

Made in the USA
Coppell, TX
28 February 2022

74233530R00085